# ATTORNEYS CAN LIE IN PENNSYLVANIA COURTS

## ACCORDING TO THE DISCIPLINARY BOARD OF THE SUPREME COURT OF PENNSYLVANIA

BEN WOOD JOHNSON

EDITED BY
WOLDEN OLIVIER

TESKO

Tesko Publishing
General Editor: Wolden Olivier

This book is published in English, Spanish, and French. The manuscript went through a rigorous editing process.

ISBN-13: 978-1-948600-95-8
ISBN-10: 1-948600-95-1

The first edition was printed in 2025 (printed in the United States)

Translated and edited by Ben Wood Johnson

Format: Pocket Book (Paperback)

www.teskopublishing.com

If you want to know more about Tesko Publishing, contact BWEC LLC/My Eduka Solutions at: 330 W. Main St # 214, Middletown, PA 17057, USA

*For my Family*
*We are under siege in Pennsylvania since 2005*

# CONTENTS

# DISCLAIMER

The book contains information and contents that reflect true events. These events took place between 2023 and 2025. This book was compiled and released to the public in the interest of accountability, transparency, and public interest. The parties involved in this case are acting in bad faith. The truth is the only cure to the false narrative that has been echoed about the nature of the misconduct of the individuals involved. See the author statement to learn more about the nature of the publication and the evidence presented in support of the our claims.

# PROLOGUE

The story of Germine Oliver (described here as G. Oliver) is not just a personal tragedy; it is a case study of the systemic failures that plague higher education and the legal system. Powerful institutions, such as Penn State University, shield themselves from accountability. Students who dare to think that they can challenge discrimination and retaliation must navigate a labyrinth of procedural violations and institutional bias.

As a doctoral student at Penn State's Ross and Carol Nese College of Nursing, Oliver faced a cascade of injustices that began with a discriminatory act. This experience culminated in her unlawful dismissal on January 31, 2024, by the very individuals she named in her discrimination complaint about three weeks earlier. However, Oliver's fight to hold the university accountable revealed a deeply entrenched system, which is dubbed here, but also echoed elsewhere, as the "Pennsylvania Corruption Machine."[1] This lethal machinery is designed to

---

1.  See the book titled: The Pennsylvania Corruption Machine" to learn more about the concept of widespread corrupt practices to protect powerful entities across Pennsylvania.

protect the powerful at the expense of the vulnerable. This is particularly true for minority and immigrant students, many of whom often lack the resources and connections to fight back.

The first layer of systemic failure in Oliver's case lies in higher education itself, where universities like Penn State often prioritize their reputation and institutional interests over fairness and equity for students. The second layer is the blatant reality of institutional corruption that makes higher education in America a subject of ridicule among developed countries. In this case, several institutions, notably the department of education itself, professional board licensing, and accreditation bodies, such as the Middle States Commission on Higher Education (MSCHE), the Pennsylvania Attorney General's Office, and other related state agencies, have joined forces with the university to smear Oliver. These institutions aimed to discourage any attempts to pursue justice. This reality is emblematic of a rotten culture designed to prevent accountability. They did things that went against the very principles of education and support that students should expect when they need them most.

The Pennsylvania corruption machine was actively working to neutralize Oliver in this case. A wide array of state agencies got involved in the matter with the sole purpose of neutralizing the threat, which they saw in Oliver and her family. I, Dr. Benjamin Johnson, the author of this book, Oliver's husband, became her only advocate in a sea of deceitful actors, many of whom were determined to find my flaws and sought to take me down personally, professionally, and psychologically.

What happened in this case? It is a critical question that underscores failures at multiple levels, from the individual to institutional and systemic failures. The repercussions of these actions extend far beyond one student. It highlights a prevalent issue within the educational and legal system.

I hope you are not the type to view skepticism toward government officials as conspiratorial in nature. In fact, the government rarely tells the truth. If [and when] they do tell the truth, it is likely because the verity [itself] may fit a particular narrative or it may satisfy a particular political objective. The book's aim is not to convince you that the commonwealth of Pennsylvania is evil. The aim is to let you [the reader] come up with your own assessment of the state's conduct in this case.

As one of the parties affected by the situation narrated in this edition, I feel obligated to share my understanding of the case with the public. This case lays bare, and in the most explicit manner, the reality of retaliation in higher education across Pennsylvania. It certainly relates to how state institutions collide to protect one another, which provides offenders with a sense of immunity to harm vulnerable individuals at will, as they know their conduct will remain unpunished.

As the author of this title, I want to share the truth about this case as candidly as possible. Keep in mind that this book is not fictional. It is based on real incidents and real decisions. In the same way, the story told here reflects my knowledge and understanding of what transpired between 2023 and 2025. But the discussion outlined in these pages, I must also admit, is based on a hypothetical rendering of how the case could have been appealed in a court of law, seemingly had it not become clear to us that this was a losing battle.

— *Benjamin Wood Johnson*
Elizabethtown, Pennsylvania (August 2025)

# THE GENESIS OF THE ABUSE

Since late 2022, Pennsylvania State University, particularly the nursing school, has engaged in a targeted campaign against Germine Oliver [G. Oliver], a female immigrant student, which later extended to her entire family, notably her husband and her children. University officials orchestrated a series of behaviors designed to discredit the family. Retaliation against family members was unfathomable, particularly during the unlawful detention of their son, Wolden Oliver, at Fort Jackson, which is a military base where school officials have professional ties.

The university also employed a range of tactics such as intimidation, libel, defamation, blatant lies, misrepresentation of events related to its actions and the situation, and straightforward fraud. The initial goal was to discredit me, Dr. Johnson, as a way to undermine my credibility. When I resisted, they went after the family relentlessly. But they did so at all costs and regardless of their own laws. Over time, other aims included attempts to deny us a voice, which ultimately denied us justice.

As will become apparent as you read through this short compilation, the university, through various school officials, notably deans, associate deans, assistant deans, faculty, and university administrators, among others, targeted a student from a protected class. They had a well-crafted plan to do their deeds and to get away with it. However, they did not expect the resistance and resilience they encountered in the family's quest for justice, which surprised them and led them to seek more sinister avenues to neutralize family members' advocacy and by denying them legal representation and any form of legal relief. This reality was like a David and Goliath moment, as it became evident that powerful forces joined together to crush a poor immigrant family under the color of state law and state power.

When Oliver's ordeal began, I, Dr. Benjamin Johnson, became the family's sole defender. At the time, I was an adjunct faculty member at the university, a position that allowed me to initially reach out to school officials to ask for help. But they removed me from the adjunct pool, which ultimately provided them with the necessary pathways they needed to continue harming Ms. Oliver, my spouse, and my confidant for more than three decades.

The university acted in complete disregard for its policies, rules, and laws. University officials acted with the utmost zeal to harm Ms. Oliver. This conduct was rewarded by state officials who condone the university's actions. Penn State university acted with complete impunity against a student who reported discrimination and retaliation. They did so without any form of penalty or consequences for their conduct.

I must note that state power meets the sheer wit and fortitude of one immigrant family. Although my wife and I are immigrants from the Caribbean, we have been living in the United States since the mid-1990s, particularly for my wife, who initially arrived in America as a lawful resident in 1996. I settled permanently in the country in the early 2000s after settling in Mexico as a medical student.

The people who targeted us were extremely powerful. Their level of confidence in their ability to harm us became increasingly obvious. They acted in complete impunity despite our numerous calls for restraint and fairness. It was as if they felt untouchable.

Among the people who targeted us include the president of the university, Neili Bendapoudi; the dean of the nursing school, Laurie Badzek; the associate dean of the nursing school, Judith Hupcey, whose family seems to have strong political ties with the governor of the state, Josh Shapiro; the program head, Sheri Matter; an assistant dean in the nursing department, a retired Army Colonel, Kelly Wolgast, an assistant dean as well, whose reputation as a tough, if not a ruthless, person preceded her; and a well-connected dean of Diversity and Equity, Stephanie Dannette Preston.

Other individuals involved in the situation included the then Secretary of Education, Khalid N. Mumin; the Executive Director of the Pennsylvania Human Relations Commission (PHRC), Chad Dion Lassiter; and a powerful law firm, Buchanan Ingersoll & Rooney PC, George Charles Morrison, Andrew Thomas Simmons, and Keith Michael Lee, among others. This list would later increase, as state agencies sided with the university and their friends to our detriment.

As an immigrant family from a French-speaking country, with English as our third and even fourth language, we faced the overwhelming power of the State of Pennsylvania alone. Still, we had been driven by our survival instincts and determination. Of course, the truth was also on our side, as the case is well documented, including emails, photos, audios, transcripts, notes, and video conversations that proved the university's misconduct and the transgression of its allies.

Despite our strong case, authentic documentation, well-worded complaints, and evidence-based claims, the university, through its trusted political allies, activated the "Pennsylvania corruption machine" to go after us, the very people they victimized. This statement is not an exaggeration. Rather—as will be apparent and as you read further—this is an accurate description of how multiple institutions, notably the Pennsylvania Disciplinary Board, Penn State University, the Pennsylvania Human Relations Commission (PHRC), local police, and even federal liaisons, like the OCR and SPPO, enlisted themselves to defeat the family by engaging in the following activities.

1. Coordinating Responses
2. Suppressing Evidence
3. Retaliation against protected activity
4. Deliberately avoiding accountability

The Oliver-Johnson family has faced a rogue university and a closed system of institutional actors protecting each other, not because the facts are unclear, but because the truth would expose them all. The signs of systemic corruption are irrefutable in this case. They include the following:

1. Cover-up instead of Investigation
2. Fabricated procedural hurdles (e.g., POA demands)
3. Delay tactics without legal basis.
4. Retaliation against lawful complaint activity

There is a need for coordination between state and federal actors to address and resolve any complaints related to the case. The reluctance to make decisions stems from the possibility of unintended consequences.

This case illustrates the Pennsylvania corruption machine in action. It epitomizes a series of bad faith actors, which form a network of personal and political interests. They grind forward to crush anything that threatens the machine's continuity. This case also exposes something that they never expected anyone to piece together. As a result, they are now reacting like a machine with no off switch, only defensive programming.

Their conduct amounts to nothing short of a well-oiled machine designed to perform a specific task. In this context, the task is to shield the machine from public exposure. Oliver's case threatened the very existential nature of the Pennsylvania corruption machine. They have been in full defensive mode.

# PART ONE
# COUNTERING THE NARRATIVE

## THE TRUTH, NOTHING BUT THE TRUTH

# CHAPTER I
# THE STORY

SINCE NOVEMBER 2022, Pennsylvania State University officials had their sights on G. Oliver, a student from the Caribbean. She had been a student in the DNP (Doctor of Nursing Practice) program since 2018. They devised a plan to remove her from the program, which came to fruition in early February 2023.

By then, Oliver had already completed all the required benchmarks for program completion, excluding her final oral presentation. However, school officials were determined to find a way or to come up with a compelling academic avenue to dismiss the student. A week before her scheduled final oral presentation, the university canceled Oliver's final stage in the program and demanded that she redo the final project, a three-semester capstone, which is guided by a program chair.

Although Oliver initially agreed to redo the project, she reached out to other school officials, including the graduate school, and raised concerns about unfair treatment. It became evident to both Oliver and I [Dr. Johnson] that the demand to complete the project did not align with school policies.[1] This

---

1.   The DNP project is divided in three courses. They include Implementation,

outreach led to a series of retaliatory actions, which led Oliver to receive a failing grade in an independent course, which was supposed to be ungraded and designed for the student to complete her project.

The DNP project is divided into three courses, labeled NURS835. The course follows a sequence of three-semester enrollment courses that students must complete consecutively. The three courses are rigorous, didactic, instructor-led, and pedagogically structured. The goal is to evaluate specific skills and precise competence. Individually, the courses contain the following phases: implementation (first semester), evaluation (second semester), and dissemination (third semester).

Each phase of the project is independent. Students must pass the phases separately to move on to the next. Upon completion of the last phase, Oliver would present her findings in an oral presentation. Upon successful completion thereof, Oliver would be allowed to graduate from the DNP program.

Oliver completed all three required phases of NURS835. However, right before her scheduled oral presentation, the project chair, Assistant Dean Sheri Matter, abruptly canceled Oliver's presentation and demanded that she redo aspects of the project she had already completed, notably during the implementation phase. The demand in itself was troubling, since the student had completed and passed the relevant phase with an A in the 2022 Summer semester.

After consulting several faculty members, Oliver filed a verbal complaint with the graduate school and other relevant university officials against the program director/project chair. She criticized the "lack of support" of her current committee.

---

evaluation, and dissemination. Each phase of the project is independent, and student must pass the phases separately to move forward and ultimately graduate. student had already completed

Oliver enlisted the help of a former academic advisor who was willing to help her clear the last hurdle and graduate from the program.

Oliver requested a re-evaluation of her case; she demanded a new project chair, her former project advisor, and new committee members. The nursing school agreed to let Oliver reconstitute a new committee. But they categorically rejected the idea that the student could have a new project chair. They also emphasized the need to select the individual who will spearhead the project.

Oliver asserted the need for a new project chair and an independent study to guarantee a fair outcome in the academic process. Although the university agreed with the latter demand, they categorically refuted the former. They insisted on their discretion to constitute the doctoral committee and not the student. Oliver felt cornered at that point. It also became clear that the university had a plan in motion and only specific individuals could carry it out.

Given that Oliver had completed all the required coursework and other requirements in the program and only needed to complete her oral presentation, she agreed to move forward. Oliver decided to ignore the university's reluctance to let her former advisor lead her project until her graduation. The student specifically requested the independent study in some specific terms, including that she should not be concerned with grading and faculty retaliation. Her goal, she insisted, was to complete her project paper and reschedule her oral presentation in the fall of 2023 to graduate.

# CHAPTER 2

# ACADEMIC CONFUSION

TWO WEEKS after the university agreed that Oliver would be enrolled in an independent study to complete her project paper, school officials reneged on that initial agreement. The program director emailed Oliver and asked why she had not registered for N835, a course that she had already completed and passed. Oliver did not understand the purpose of the request. She asked to speak to the director of the program.

The program director agreed to speak with the student. During a phone call conversation, the director asserted that if Oliver did not register for N835, she would be dismissed from the program. When Oliver insisted on having more clarification about the reason that she had to retake a course she had already completed, given that the university had already committed to an independent study course, the program director reiterated threats about program dismissal and abruptly hung up the phone.

Having witnessed the behavior of the program director, which I found unprofessional and unethical, I, an adjunct faculty at the university at the time, reached out to the university president and formally filed a complaint against the nursing school. I asked university officials to intervene in the matter. Soon after my complaint, an ethics compliance officer, Tabitha Oman, reached back to me and wanted to speak directly with Oliver.

Oliver reached out to the ethics compliance officer; they set up a meeting to discuss the problem. During that meeting, it was understood that an independent study course was the only way forward, given Oliver's academic status. Oliver had met all academic requirements by then. There was no mechanism that the school could use to force Oliver to retake a course she had already taken and passed.

For the second time, the university, the DNP program officials, and the nursing school [as a whole] agreed that Oliver would enroll in the independent study for the upcoming fall semester. The independent study course would be designed as N596, which is a type of course that can be offered on an individual basis, as students may need to further their research skills on a particular subject or topic. The goal was for Oliver to complete her project paper.

The independent study course, which Oliver requested in specific terms, was approved as requested. The sole purpose of the new course, as school officials echoed in emails and other communications, was for Oliver to complete her project paper. Soon thereafter, she could make her oral presentation. Once the project paper is approved, preferably at the end of the semester, Oliver could graduate. Until the project paper is finalized and the final oral presentation scheduled, school officials said that Oliver must repeat the course; she must do so until the paper has been approved.

The university chose Kelly Wolgast, a retired army colonel with a rough reputation, to oversee Oliver's project paper. From the start, it was clear that the university had brought in a tough individual to handle the situation, which was not necessarily in

Oliver's interest. Perhaps the goal was to tame Oliver or to quell any dissent on her part.

Although the project chair [course instructor as well] and Oliver had a rough start, since the army colonel refused to meet with the student outside of her own meeting terms, Oliver, under my supervision, agreed to accept the demands of the new course instructor. She agreed to abide by any demands related to providing proof of all the work that she completed. For a while, everything seemed to go well.

The course instructor/project chair was satisfied with the documentation that Oliver presented, which proved that the initial project was conducted in accordance with school policy, comps/proposal specifications, and the expectations laid out by the previous project chair and program director. After a few more Zoom meetings, the new project chair expressed her satisfaction with what Oliver had already accomplished. She confirmed that Oliver completed the project in accordance with program expectations. The project chair asked Oliver to initiate the graduation process by informing the graduate school of her formal intention to graduate in the fall of 2023, the current semester.

As everything seemed in place for Oliver to complete the program, the paper revision process had begun. The new project chair said that Oliver can proceed with making the necessary corrections on her project paper. However, revisions had to follow a specific regimen, as initially understood. At that point, Oliver and the new project chair/course instructor agreed to move forward and to continue revising the paper until it was good enough to present to other committee members for their review and to schedule her final oral presentation.

The main reasons for the independent study course were paper revision and oral presentation, which had been spaced out in different periods and time frames until a decision could be made whether Oliver could present her final paper for review and schedule her project presentation at the end of the semester. The instructor set up a mechanism to evaluate Oliver's paper writing progress. However, something had changed in the timeline, or some new issue had been introduced in the fray.

As the semester progressed, the instructor's attitude became increasingly hostile toward Oliver. She seemed more evasive and indecisive. By mid-semester, the instructor ordered Oliver to send a copy of her project paper to other committee members, signaling her satisfaction with the document, as she initially said that she would have Oliver send the finished paper draft to committee members only when the paper was ready for review.

The review process from other committee members lasted longer than usual. It was as if they were stalling on some specific date. They waited until a week (in one case, a few days) before the scheduled presentation to send their feedback to Oliver. Their comments were vague. They did not address the document substantively.

While Oliver worked arduously to make the recommended corrections suggested by the instructor in the document, the course instructor still canceled Oliver's oral presentation. Oliver protested the decision. But the instructor changed the nature of the course toward the end of the semester into a graded course anyway. The instructor told Oliver that if she did not do as she demanded, she would be dismissed from the program.

In the days after the project presentation cancellation, Oliver engaged with the course instructor and demanded clarifications on the reason for the cancellation. However, the course instructor kept framing her response as if to suggest that Oliver was academically deficient. It became clear that the university was crafting a narrative against Oliver and had already made decisions. They were now attempting to contextualize their actions through an academic framework.

I helped Oliver craft several emails to the school. We argued that any deficiencies should not be Oliver's fault. We emphasized that any obstacles that the student faced came from the university itself. We also underlined that Oliver should not be penalized for conduct induced and entrenched by the university or school officials.

The course instructor called Oliver's academic integrity into question. She expressed doubts about the execution of the initial project. She questioned whether the people Oliver listed as participants existed or were made up. The instructor demanded proof that the project was carried out as stated. Once again, Oliver provided all the required information. But the course instructor insisted that Oliver was academically deficient.

After abruptly canceling Oliver's oral presentation for the second time, the course instructor became increasingly aggressive in her actions and behavior toward the student. She kept making demands that, even when Oliver agreed to them, were not enough. Once again, the course instructor demanded that Oliver redo the entire project, not just the paper, as originally understood.

Oliver, on my cautious advice, understood what was being prepared. But she agreed to redo the project, as requested. Oliver also noted that the demands were unrealistic, as she was asked to redo portions of the project that took her three semesters to complete in less than a month. Oliver further noted that she no longer had access to the site she initially used for the study, a site that was approved specifically for the project.

The course instructor acknowledged that the loss of the site was a major hurdle. She also made more demands; she increased prior ones. It was as if the course instructor wanted

Oliver to voice a clear disagreement with her demands. Surprisingly, the instructor failed Oliver in the independent study course, which, as noted earlier and based on clearly communicated email conversations, was supposed to be ungraded. Oliver received an F grade for the course, ostensibly after claiming the course instructor's conduct amounted to harassment, retaliation, and intimidation.

# CHAPTER 3

# THE COMPLAINTS

On January 2, 2024, Oliver filed a discrimination complaint with Penn State's Affirmative Action Office. She argued that several administrators and faculty members in the College of Nursing had discriminated against her. University officials initially acknowledged the complaint. However, school officials, via the affirmative action office, decided to isolate Oliver.

School officials asked Oliver not to contact program officials, presumably for her own good. I felt that the university's demand was a strategic move. I thought this was a cynical trick designed to contain the situation and ultimately dismiss Oliver with the blessing of a fake investigation, which would have yielded a verdict that the university did nothing wrong.

On January 24, 2024, Oliver had formally requested a grade adjudication for her N596 independent study (Fall 2023). But Judith Hupcey, the administrator who was also responsible for grade adjudication and a person that was named in Oliver's discrimination complaint, ignored this request. Just 29 days later, on January 31, 2024, that same administrator—who was not a member of Oliver's doctoral committee—issued the student dismissal, citing academic performance as the reason.

The administrator then used the failing grade from the independent study course, which had not been adjudicated despite numerous requests, as a basis or pretext to dismiss Oliver from the program.

The firing and actions taken by university officials went against Penn State's own rules (GCAC-803), which clearly say that only a doctoral committee can decide to dismiss a doctoral student for poor scholarship, and that the final decision must be made by the Dean of the Fox Graduate School. The unilateral action bypassed both requirements, which denied Oliver advance notice, an opportunity for review, and the procedural protections guaranteed by the policy noted.

In a formal response to the PHRC, the university claimed that it dismissed Oliver for academic reasons and had "robust" policies in place. The university, through its attorneys (George Charles Morrison, Andrew Thomas Simmons, and Keith Michael Lee), clearly perjured themselves about Oliver's grade adjudication request on January 24, 2024. Although the school claimed that the dismissal was based on academic reasons, Oliver was dismissed for a course that was supposed to be non-graded, as she completed all required courses in the program. Similarly, Oliver was not provided with the opportunity to be heard, as per school policies.

This violation was compounded by the obvious due process failure. Grade adjudication only occurred post-dismissal, after dismissal, and after Oliver's reinstatement, confirming that the grade was not final at the time of dismissal, a clear violation of due process, as students are entitled to a fair opportunity to challenge academic decisions before adverse actions are taken. The administrator's conflict of interest, combined with the close temporal proximity between the discrimination complaint and the dismissal, demonstrated that the action was likely retaliatory and not academic.

The university dismissed Oliver just days after her formal grade adjudication request. But they did so without addressing the pending adjudication. The cover-up that followed was even more problematic, as several state and federal entities and officials lined up to undermine Oliver and her family at every turn.

Not only did the university cite course failure as the basis for Oliver's dismissal, but the dean of the nursing school, Laurie Badzek, also made a false statement about Oliver's academic progress and her record. The dean cited a nonexistent course number (N685) to justify the academic dismissal. When Oliver challenged the false information about her academic records, the university remained silent. The school later refused to make corrections or even allow Oliver to view her records under FERPA.

Oliver filed several complaints with state and federal officials. However, these complaints were dismissed or referred to the PHRC for adjudication. Oliver also discovered that Chad Dion Lassiter, the Executive Director of the PHRC, engaged publicly with the university just days after she indicated her intention to contact the agency in a formal email to Stephanie Dannette Preston, the Dean of Equity.

In January 2024, Oliver and her family contacted the PHRC; they filed a verbal complaint against the university, just one month before Lassiter's involvement with Penn State in an official banquet in February 2024. Mr. Lassiter gave a keynote address at the university during the 2024 Martin Luther King, Jr. Commemorative Banquet at Penn State Harrisburg. However, despite the PHRC's initial involvement in Oliver's case and their knowledge of an impending issue with the university, Mr. Lassiter did not recuse himself from the case either before and after the official banquet, even though Oliver continued to reach out to the agency before, during, and even after Lassiter's engagement with the institution, which the agency has a mandate to investigate upon the receipt of legitimate complaint.

Despite all the evidentiary documents presented, the PHRC, through its executive director, Chad Dion Lassiter, endorsed the university's version of events, including making an additional false statement about Oliver's academic record. For example, the agency stated that Oliver had received two grades below a B as of May 2023, which is demonstrably false, according to Oliver's transcript. When Oliver and her family insisted on Mr. Lassiter's recusal of the case, the agency targeted the family with legal threats and engaged in retaliatory conduct, including their refusal to investigate other complaints from family members and imposed POA demands.

As will be apparent in the following chapters, Oliver faced enormous pushbacks from the university and later from state and federal officials. However, the focus here is the conduct of the Pennsylvania Disciplinary Board, as they epitomize the notion of a corruption machine. The members of the Pennsylvania Disciplinary Board acted with little to no shame in expressing views that they knew, or have reasons to know, conflict with their core mission to safeguard professional conduct in the legal profession.

The Pennsylvania Disciplinary Board went all the way against the Oliver-Johnson family in this case. They disclosed to anyone who might be interested that they were not acting as an impartial arbitrator in this case, as one of the attorneys involved worked for the Court and presumably had strong ties with board officials. Thus, they have a personal stake in the outcome. Accordingly, the phrase "facing the Pennsylvania corruption machine" is not only valid in the present context. But it also proves a truth that will hopefully become undeniable as you read this text and examine the evidence at the end of the manuscript.

The disciplinary board deliberately invoked confidentiality to limit any discussion about their behavior. As the author of this book, I, Benjamin Wood Johnson, take full responsibility for publishing this work, given my knowledge of the events that transpired. I can't stay quiet as those in power abuse their power to the detriment of those who have no voice.

As one of the parties affected by the situation narrated here, I feel obligated to be ashamed of my understanding of the case with the public. This case lays bare, and in the most explicit manner, the reality of retaliation in higher education across the Commonwealth of Pennsylvania. It certainly relates to how state institutions collide to protect one another, which provides offenders with a sense of immunity to harm vulnerable individuals at will. They know that their conduct will remain unpunished.

# CHAPTER 4
# THE PENNSYLVANIA CORRUPTION MACHINE

In the labyrinth of Penn State's defense against Oliver's allegations, the Pennsylvania Supreme Court Disciplinary Board emerged as yet another gatekeeper in what I've come to call the "Pennsylvania Corruption Machine"—which could be understood as a system of institutional protection that shields powerful entities from accountability, even when their misconduct is undeniable.

On October 8, 2024, the Board dismissed Oliver's complaints against Buchanan Ingersoll & Rooney PC attorneys George Charles Morrison, Esq. [File # C1-24-723], Andrew Thomas Simmons, Esq. [File # C1-24-724], and Keith Michael Lee, Esq. [File # C1-24-725]),[1] who represented Penn State in the Pennsylvania Human Relations Commission (PHRC) proceedings. See the complaints towards the end of the manuscript. This dismissal, despite unambiguous evidence of the attorneys' misrepresentation, was a stark illustration of how the system bends to protect its own, thereby leaving students like Oliver,

---

1. These numbers were assigned to the attorneys by the Pennsylvania Supreme Court Disciplinary Board for the formal complaint.

who dare to challenge discrimination and retaliation, to fight an uphill battle against an impenetrable wall of institutional power.

## THE COMPLAINT

Oliver's complaints to the Disciplinary Board were rooted in a blatant falsehood presented by the attorneys in their formal response to the PHRC. The attorneys claimed that the student —Oliver—"had not requested a grade adjudication prior to her January 31, 2024, academic dismissal letter from the College of Nursing." See attached exhibits towards the end of the manuscript. This statement was not a mere oversight; it was a deliberate misrepresentation of the facts, given that the very email the attorneys referenced specifically stated that they are responding to the student's grade adjudication request, which will be allowed post-facto dismissal.

Such misrepresentations can have serious implications for all parties involved. False statements compromise the integrity of the disciplinary process. Clarity and truthfulness in such matters are essential to a fair resolution.

## THE EVIDENCE

On January 24, 2024, Oliver had emailed a formal request for a grade adjudication for her N596 independent study (Fall 2023) to multiple university offices, including the administrator responsible for grade adjudication (who was also named in her January 2, 2024, discrimination complaint), the Grad Dean's Office, and others. The email, with an attached document formalizing the request, was a clear and undeniable record of her action, sent seven days before her dismissal.

The attorneys asserted otherwise about the facts

surrounding the dismissal. In doing so, they obscured the procedural violation at the heart of Oliver's dismissal. The critical issue was that Penn State had terminated her without addressing her pending grade adjudication. This was a direct violation of due process and university policy, thereby raising fundamental questions about the fairness of the dismissal process.

## COMPLAINT DISMISSED

The Disciplinary Board's response to this clear evidence of misconduct was truly remarkable. In their letter on 8 October 2024, signed by Disciplinary Counsel Dana M. Pirone, the Board acknowledged Oliver's complaint but also categorically dismissed it. They claimed they could not "substantiate a violation of the Rules of Professional Conduct based upon [her] allegations."

The Board argued that its jurisdiction was limited to enforcing the Rules of Professional Conduct (RPC), a set of minimum ethical standards for attorneys. They emphasized that not all "unprofessional" or "unethical" conduct violates these rules. Furthermore, they stated that they could only discipline attorneys for conduct that "clearly violates a specific rule."

The Board further highlighted that any clear violation must be established by a "preponderance of the evidence." According to the Board, the misrepresentation did not meet this threshold. This conclusion raised questions about the effectiveness of the Disciplinary Board in addressing serious allegations of attorney misconduct.

## A SYSTEM DESIGNED TO SUPPRESS RIGHTS

Pennsylvania government is known for their corruption practices. What we are confronting in the Commonwealth of Pennsylvania is not a mere lapse in institutional integrity, a
bureaucratic misstep, or an isolated case of mismanagement. It
is a meticulously constructed wall and fully operational corruption machine, a sophisticated network of interlocking entities
that, under the guise of public service, perpetuate systemic
abuse, shields wrongdoing, and silences dissent.

This machine is not an accident; it is a deliberate apparatus.
It is engineered to protect powerful institutions and their allies
while crushing those who dare challenge its authority.

Entities such as a prestigious public university (Penn State),
a civil rights enforcement agency (the Pennsylvania Human
Relations Commission, or PHRC), state-connected police forces,
local municipalities, and even federal oversight bodies like the
Office for Civil Rights (OCR) and the Student Privacy Policy
Office (SPPO) are at the heart of the situation. These institutions have also abandoned their mandates. They colluded to
orchestrate a campaign of harassment, retaliation, and
suppression against a Black immigrant family in Elizabethtown, Pennsylvania.

This is not a story of isolated civil rights enforcement failures, but a chilling exposé of a coordinated system designed to
deny justice, evade accountability, and outlast its victims. The
implications of this failure extend beyond individual cases; they
threaten the integrity of the democratic process itself. By
ignoring their responsibilities, these entities have undermined
public trust in systems meant to protect and serve Pennsylvania
communities, notably marginalized groups and individuals
from protected classes.

Let us name, openly, the very thing, or corruption, that state authorities, notably the Pennsylvania Disciplinary Board, refused to acknowledge. It is imperative to shine a light on these injustices to foster accountability and ensure that no family must endure such treatment in silence. However, I must admit ii here as well, only through recognition and action can a path toward justice be forged for those affected.

# PART TWO
# THE PA
# DISCIPLINARY
# BOARD IN THEIR
# OWN WORDS

SEE THE IMAGES [AS EVIDENCE]
ATTACHED TOWARDS THE END OF
THE BOOK

# CHAPTER 5

# THE DISMISSAL LETTER OF THE DISCIPLINARY BOARD (LIGHTLY EDITED)

DEAR Ms. Oliver:

After reviewing the complaints against George Charles Morrison, Esquire, Andrew Thomas Simmons, Esquire, and Keith Michael Lee, Esquire, our office has determined that the complaints warrant dismissal for the reasons stated below.

In the complaints, you state, among other things, that Mr. Morrison, Mr. Simmons, and Mr. Lee are the opposing attorneys in your Pennsylvania Human Relations Commission (PHRC) matter against Penn State Ross and Carol Nese College of Nursing No. 202317185. Your complaint to the PHRC concerns whether you did or did not submit a formal request for a grade adjudication prior to the issuance of the January 31, 2024, academic dismissal letter. You state that you emailed the formal request on January 24, 2024; however, the attorneys take a different position in their client's formal response on July 15, 2024. Thus, you believe that the record in the PHRC proceedings does not accurately represent the factual circumstances as to your January 24, 2024, submission. You ask that this office, among other things, direct the attorneys to retract the false statements and information they provided to the PHRC.

The Rules of Professional Conduct are limited in scope, and express specific prohibitions in limited areas of what might be called "improper" or "unethical" behavior. Some actions which one might consider "improper" or "unethical" do not violate any of the pertinent Rules. An attorney can only be disciplined for conduct that clearly violates a specific Rule. Moreover, this office must assess matters complained of as to whether any clear disciplinary violation involved is established by a preponderance of the evidence. Although we appreciate your frustration as you have described it, because we cannot substantiate a violation of the RULES of Professional Conduct based upon your allegations, we have dismissed the complaints.

At the outset, it is important for you to know some limitations on this office's consideration of the disciplinary complaints. Our jurisdiction and authority are limited to attempting to enforce the Rules of Professional Conduct, a set of minimum ethical standards with which all attorneys must abide. While the Rules are quite broad in their scope, they simply do not prohibit all conduct by an attorney which might be considered as unprofessional, inappropriate, or "unethical."

Moreover, even though you have submitted complaints, this office does not represent you or your personal interests in the PHRC matter. We are not your attorney and cannot provide you with any personal legal advice. We cannot attempt to obtain any remedy or damages you feel you are entitled to nor can we interfere or intervene in any pending or future legal proceedings you might be involved.

As counsel for the opposing party, the attorneys have a duty to pursue their client's interests, which may naturally oppose your interests. The vast majority of the Rules of Professional Conduct pertain to the attorney-client relationship. The attorneys do not have a duty to you under the Rules such as an attorney would have to a client, including the duty to pursue and protect the interests of anyone other than their client. They are not obligated to act in your direction or in accordance with your demands.

The issues you raise regarding the validity of facts or positions asserted by the attorneys in matters you have pending before the PHRC involve issues of fact and law that are more appropriate for that tribunal to consider and determine. This office is not the forum in which to challenge the opposing position presented by the attorneys. Thus, your concerns are more appropriately raised before the PHRC or tribunal for review and resolution, not this office.

It is not the role or function of this office to make determinations of law or facts, nor to second-guess any such determinations as may be made by a tribunal. Simply put, this office cannot make determinations of law or fact in this underlying matter, nor do we have the authority or jurisdiction to impact or otherwise review determinations made by a tribunal.

If you have ongoing concerns, you should consult with counsel of your choosing who can advise you as to any clear rights, remedies, and options you may have to pursue your concerns concerning the PHRC matter.

That said, if in the course of the litigation there is a specific, written finding made by the PHRC or a court that any of the attorneys committed misconduct with respect to the matters about which you complain, you may contact this office at that time and provide us with a copy of the finding or opinion so that we may evaluate the matter further in light of that finding. It remains the responsibility of the Disciplinary Counsel, the Disciplinary Board, and the Supreme Court to determine whether to bring formal disciplinary charges against an attorney. We do not have the authority to set aside or modify the actions of the tribunal. With few exceptions, unless the Office of Disciplinary Counsel files formal charges, the disciplinary matter remains confidential and the respondent-attorney is not required to answer to the complainant.

# CHAPTER 6

# RESPONSE TO PA DISCIPLINARY BOARD

DEAR MS. DANA M. PIRONE,

I am writing to formally express my serious concerns regarding the handling and dismissal of my complaints against attorneys George Charles Morrison, Andrew Thomas Simmons, and Keith Michael Lee. After carefully reviewing the correspondence sent by Ms. Dana M. Pirone on October 9, 2024, it has become clear that the Board's decision to dismiss my complaints reflects significant contradictions, ethical missteps, and a failure to adhere to the standards of impartial oversight that the Disciplinary Board is entrusted to uphold.

The law considers any knowingly false statement made under oath as a serious offense, particularly when it impacts legal proceedings. Under 18 U.S.C. § 1621, perjury can lead to fines and imprisonment for up to five years if proven. The definition includes testimony and written statements presented under oath, where the individual willfully provides false information on a material matter. This can also extend to statements made in written documents if they are submitted with the understanding that they must be truthful, as required in legal settings.

Likewise, making false statements in an official court proceeding or in communications with a tribunal is universally recognized as unethical under various codes of conduct, especially in legal practice. The ethical standards that govern attorneys—such as Rule 3.3 (Candor Toward the Tribunal) and Rule 4.1 (Truthfulness in Statements to Others)—explicitly prohibit this type of behavior. It is not a matter of interpretation or subjective judgment; the rule is clear and objective. The attorneys, by submitting false statements in response to the Pennsylvania Human Relations Commission (PHRC), violated these established rules.

**1. Contradictions in Authority and the Determination of Violations.** The Board's letter claims that it does not have the authority to make factual or legal determinations regarding the case, yet simultaneously concludes that no violation of the Rules of Professional Conduct occurred. This contradiction is deeply troubling, as it raises serious questions about the integrity of the Board's decision-making process.

If the Disciplinary Board lacks the authority to assess facts or evidence, how can it dismiss a complaint based on those very same facts? By claiming both to lack authority and to reach a definitive conclusion, the Board is engaging in circular reasoning, which not only undermines its credibility but also prevents a fair evaluation of the evidence I provided.

Additionally, the letter suggests that I may contact the Board again if a "specific, written finding" of attorney misconduct is made by an external body, such as the PHRC or a court. If the Board is claiming it lacks authority now, why would this change be based on an external ruling? This recommendation further contradicts the stated limitations of the Board's authority and calls into question the consistency and fairness of its approach to enforcement.

**2. Tolerance of Potentially Unethical Conduct.** The letter acknowledges that the attorneys "took a different position" regarding the facts of my case and suggests that their conduct was permissible because they were pursuing their client's interests. While attorneys are obligated to advocate for their clients, they are equally bound by the Rules of Professional Conduct, including Rule 3.3 (Candor Toward the Tribunal) and Rule 4.1 (Truthfulness in Statements to Others). These rules explicitly prohibit attorneys from knowingly making false statements of fact or law.

By framing the attorneys' actions as merely "taking a different position," the Board's letter implicitly tolerates the potential misrepresentation of the facts. This sends a dangerous message—that attorneys can disregard truthfulness as long as it aligns with their client's interests. This attitude undermines the ethical standards that the legal profession is built upon and suggests that the Disciplinary Board is willing to condone behavior that violates the spirit and letter of the Rules of Professional Conduct.

**3. Failure to Address Key Evidence Properly.** The Board mischaracterized the nature of the evidence I provided, treating it as a mere "assertion" rather than verified documentation. Specifically, my formal email request for grade adjudication, submitted on January 24, 2024, was not just an assertion—it was a concrete piece of evidence that directly contradicts the attorneys' claims.

The Board's failure to properly examine or acknowledge this evidence raises serious concerns about the thoroughness and objectivity of the review process. Rule 3.3 and Rule 4.1 place clear obligations on attorneys to act with honesty and transparency. The dismissal of this evidence without investigation reflects a significant failure to enforce these rules, which should have triggered deeper scrutiny into the attorneys' conduct.

**4. Contradictions on Confidentiality and Scrutiny.** The

Board's insistence on the confidentiality of the disciplinary process, while typical, takes on an unusual tone in this context. When viewed alongside the contradictions in the Board's reasoning and the implicit tolerance of potentially unethical conduct, the emphasis on confidentiality appears to be more about shielding the Board's decisions from scrutiny than protecting the integrity of the process.

While confidentiality is a procedural norm, it should not be used as a tool to prevent legitimate challenges to the fairness or consistency of the Board's actions. I am fully entitled to discuss how my case was handled under the law, particularly when there are clear indications of bias, ethical missteps, or a failure to enforce the Rules of Professional Conduct.

**5. Erosion of Public Trust and Institutional Integrity.** The Disciplinary Board's role is to maintain the highest standards of ethical conduct in the legal profession. However, the handling of my complaint calls into question whether the Board is fulfilling this responsibility. By failing to thoroughly investigate clear evidence, by issuing contradictory statements about its own authority, and by implying that attorney misrepresentation is tolerable, the Board risks undermining public trust in its ability to uphold the integrity of the profession.

As a body connected to the Supreme Court of Pennsylvania, the Board should hold itself to the highest standard of impartiality and rigor. This is particularly important when dealing with complaints that involve ethical violations that may impact public confidence in the legal system.

**6. Lack of Clear Justification for the Dismissal.** There is no legitimate basis for the dismissal. The letter fails to cite specific facts, legal precedents, or applicable rules that would justify the dismissal. Instead, it relies on vague references to the attorneys "taking a different position" and the Board's supposed lack of authority, neither of which are sufficient grounds for dismissal. Without a detailed and transparent explanation of how the Board reached its conclusion, the dismissal lacks accountability and undermines the entire process. There is no clear, legitimate basis provided for why my complaint did not merit further investigation or review.

**7. Absence of Evidence-Based Evaluation.** The foundation of due process is that decisions are made based on the careful review and consideration of evidence. In this case, there is no indication that the Board engaged in a substantive evaluation of the evidence I provided. Specifically, I noted in my complaint my formal email request for grade adjudication, which directly contradicts the claims made by the attorneys. This email is a key piece of evidence that demonstrates the attorneys' misrepresentation of the facts.

Despite the noted submission to the proper school authorities, the Board's dismissal makes no reference to this email or any other evidence. The decision merely asserts that no violation of the Rules of Professional Conduct occurred but does not explain how that conclusion was reached.

Due process requires that a decision-maker provide reasoning that reflects a review of the facts. Without an explanation as to why the evidence does not support my claims, the dismissal appears arbitrary. The Board's failure to engage with the evidence constitutes a procedural deficiency that undermines the legitimacy of its decision.

**8. No Explanation or Justification for the Conclusion.** Due process demands that decisions be accompanied by a reasoned explanation that connects the facts to the relevant rules. The Board, however, failed to provide any substantive justification for its conclusion that the attorneys did not violate the Rules of Professional Conduct. The letter does not address the key issue of misrepresentation or the contradiction between

the attorneys' statements and the documented evidence I
provided.

If the Board believed that my evidence was insufficient, it
was obligated to explain why. A due process-compliant
dismissal would have involved a step-by-step explanation of:

• How the Board evaluated the evidence I provided

• Which specific rules of conduct were applied

• Why did the conduct of the attorneys not violate those
rules, based on the facts

The lack of explanation amounts to a denial of due process,
as I am left without any understanding of why the Board
dismissed my claims.

**9. Contradictions in Authority and Reasoning.** The
Board's letter contains contradictory statements that further
underscore the lack of a fair process. On the one hand, the
Board claims that it does not have the authority to determine
facts or review legal issues. On the other hand, the Board
dismissed my complaint, which inherently required making
factual and legal determinations. This contradiction not only
calls into question the fairness of the process but also raises
concerns about the legitimacy of the Board's decision.

Due process requires consistency and transparency in
reasoning. The Board cannot simultaneously claim that it lacks
authority to review facts while issuing a definitive decision that
necessarily involves assessing the very facts it claims it cannot
evaluate. This inconsistency undermines the credibility of the
entire process.

**10. Prejudgment Without a Proper Review.** The dismissal
also suggests that the Board prejudged the case without
conducting a thorough review of the facts. The conclusion
appears to have been reached without properly examining the
evidence I submitted, particularly my January 24 email. This
gives the impression that the Board's decision was made in a

manner that was not impartial or reflective of a full and fair investigation.

Due process requires fair and impartial decisions based on thorough evidence review. By failing to properly investigate the facts or provide an adequate explanation, the Board's dismissal denies me the procedural fairness that is fundamental to the disciplinary process.

**11. Lack of Engagement with the Rules of Professional Conduct.** The Board's letter asserts that the attorneys' conduct did not violate the Rules of Professional Conduct but fails to explain how that conclusion was reached. The attorneys' potential violations of Rule 3.3 (Candor Toward the Tribunal), Rule 4.1 (Truthfulness in Statements to Others), and Rule 8.4 (Misconduct) are key issues that were not addressed in the dismissal.

A proper due process review would:

• Apply the relevant rules of conduct to the specific facts of the case

• Explain why the attorneys' actions did or did not meet the threshold for a violation

• Provide a clear rationale for the decision

The failure to engage with the rules and apply them to the facts in a reasoned manner denies me due process and raises serious concerns about the Board's adherence to its responsibility as an oversight body.

**12. Confidentiality and Suppression of Accountability.** While confidentiality is a procedural norm in disciplinary processes, the Board's emphasis on confidentiality in this context appears to serve as a shield to prevent external scrutiny of a flawed process. Due process includes not only the right to a fair and impartial decision but also the right to challenge procedural deficiencies. By relying heavily on confidentiality while issuing a contradictory and unexplained dismissal, the

Board seems to be suppressing transparency rather than protecting the integrity of the process.

Due process cannot be sacrificed in the name of confidentiality. Confidentiality should not be used to obscure accountability, especially when there are clear indications that the dismissal was procedurally deficient and lacked substantive engagement with the evidence.

**Conclusion.** In reviewing the Disciplinary Board's letter, it is evident that the dismissal lacks a valid and justifiable basis. The contradictions in the Board's authority, failure to engage with the evidence, the absence of any substantive application of the relevant ethical rules, and the deferral to other tribunals all point to a decision made without thorough or proper investigation.

The dismissal is not grounded in either fact or law. The Board's reasoning is inconsistent with its role as an oversight body responsible for enforcing ethical conduct standards. This strongly suggests that the decision was not based on a fair evaluation of the merits of my complaint.

Moreover, I must respectfully assert that the Disciplinary Board's dismissal of my complaint constitutes a violation of my right to due process, given that the decision lacks the essential components of a fair and reasonable process. The dismissal of my complaint did not meet the fundamental requirements of due process, given the failure to review the evidence, the absence of a judicious explanation for the dismissal, the blatant disregard for the relevant rules, and the contradictory statements that characterized the correspondence. All these procedural deficiencies suggest that the process was not conducted in a fair or impartial manner.

I am formally resubmitting my complaint with two additional claims that have come to light since the initial filing: 1) the attorneys' false statements regarding their knowledge of my protected activities prior to January 31, 2024, and 2) the false representations made regarding the completion of my required courses. I am also providing new supporting evidence that directly contradicts the attorneys' statements in these matters. These new claims and the associated documentation are critical to understanding the full scope of the ethical violations and provide substantial grounds for reconsideration.

The Board's handling of this matter has broader implications for the enforcement of ethical standards within the legal profession. I hope that the Disciplinary Board will take this opportunity to reaffirm its commitment to fairness, impartiality, and justice. While the Board stressed confidentiality, the dismissal letter has established a precedent, which should not go unchallenged. Therefore, I request that the Board reevaluates its decision and conduct a thorough, but also impartial, review of the evidence and the claims I raised, consistent with the principles of due process. A decision based on the facts, supported by clear reasoning, and grounded in the applicable rules of professional conduct is essential to ensure that justice is served.

In light of the issues outlined above, I formally request a reconsideration of the decision to dismiss my complaints. I urge the Board to conduct a more thorough investigation into the conduct of Mr. Morrison, Mr. Simmons, and Mr. Lee, with full attention to the ethical obligations outlined in Rules 3.3, 4.1, and 8.4 of the Rules of Professional Conduct.

Should the Board choose not to reconsider this matter, I will have no choice but to seek external avenues of accountability to ensure that these ethical violations are properly addressed. My goal is to see this matter resolved in accordance with the ethical standards that govern all members of the legal community. I look forward to your prompt and thoughtful response to this request.

Sincerely,

Germine Oliver

Assisted by Benjamin W. Johnson, Ph.D.
Ben Wood Educational Consulting, LLC
330 W E Main St. #214
Middletown, PA 17057
Phone: 814-424-8816
E-mail: benjaminjson@proton.me

**CC:**
Mr. Thomas J. Farrell, Chief Disciplinary Counsel
Mr. Raymond S. Wierciszewski, Deputy Chief Disciplinary Counsel
Ms. Jana M. Palko, Counsel-in-Charge, Central Intake

# PART THREE
# THE PA DISCIPLINARY BOARD AS CORRUPT ENTITY

## THE EPITOME OF THE PENNSYLVANIA CORRUPTION MACHINE AT WORK

# CHAPTER 7

# A SHIELD FOR MISCONDUCT

THE PENNSYLVANIA DISCIPLINARY BOARD dismissed Oliver's complaint on the basis that it could not determine the validity of the issues raised due to its limitations and jurisdiction. This reasoning is baffling in light of the evidence. The Pennsylvania Rules of Professional Conduct, specifically Rule 3.3 (Candor Toward the Tribunal), explicitly require lawyers to be truthful in their representations to a tribunal or administrative body like the PHRC.

Penn State attorneys' claim that Oliver had not requested a grade adjudication was demonstrably false, as the January 24, 2024, email directly contradicted their statement. This was not a matter of interpretation or ambiguity; it was a clear false-hood, presented to the PHRC to obscure the procedural violations and retaliation that underpinned Oliver's dismissal. The evidence was not only preponderant; it was irrefutable.

The Disciplinary Board opted to dismiss the complaint, thereby ignoring the attorney's misconduct. This dismissal raises fundamental questions about the integrity of the board's decision-making process. The implications of ignoring this evidence have far-reaching consequences for the justice system and those seeking redress.

The letter went further; it emphasized that they do not represent the complainant (Oliver) and cannot intervene in the PHRC proceedings. They argued that the issues Oliver raised—the validity of the attorneys' statements to the PHRC —were "matters of fact and law" for the PHRC to determine, not the Disciplinary Board. This distinction made it clear to Oliver that her concerns would not be directly addressed by the board.

They suggested that if the PHRC or a court made a specific written finding of misconduct by the attorneys, Oliver could resubmit her complaint with that finding for further evaluation. This response created a maddening catch-22: The PHRC might not have addressed the attorneys' misconduct if the Disciplinary Board did not act. Likewise, the Board would not act without a finding from the PHRC, which led to a frustrating stalemate.

This circular reasoning ensured that the misrepresentation would go unpunished. As a result, Oliver was left to face the consequences of a tainted investigation without recourse. It placed her in a position where her concerns could never reach a resolution, thereby leaving her without any means to seek justice.

## EFFECT OF COMPLAINT DISMISSAL

The dismissal was more than a procedural setback: it was a glaring example of the "Pennsylvania corruption machine" at work. The Board's refusal to hold the attorneys accountable, despite unambiguous evidence of their violation of Rule 3.3, suggested a systemic reluctance to challenge powerful institutions such as Penn State and their well-connected legal representatives. This behavior raises concerns about the integrity of the legal system and the possibility of further abuse.

The misrepresentation was not a trivial error; it was a calculated move to mislead the PHRC or to give the latter a straightforward pathway to dismiss the complaint while the former retained a plausible deniability argument to defend its actions or inactions in this case. Their actions, nonetheless, obscured the due-process violation of dismissing Oliver without addressing her grade adjudication request.

The angle of retaliation is significant here. The Disciplinary Board acted as the attorneys' own defense lawyers. Most important, we must consider the administrator's conflict of interest in the matter. We must also examine the close temporal proximity between Oliver's discrimination complaint on January 2, 2024, and her unlawful dismissal on January 31, 2024. Somehow, the PA Disciplinary Board could see no wrong in the attorneys' conduct during the PHRC investigation. Arguably, the Board decided to pretend not to see the implications, as doing so would require a thorough analysis of the situation, which would inevitably lead to the conclusion that the statements to the PHRC were not incidental or innocent mistakes made to a tribunal.

By dismissing Oliver's complaint against the attorneys, the Disciplinary Board effectively endorsed Penn State attorney's deception, which they fed directly to the PHRC. This endorsement, coincidentally, freed Penn State from the burden of truth, thereby enabling the institution to continue its defense. The implications of such actions extend beyond this case, as it highlights a troubling trend in how institutional power can manipulate legal processes and vice versa.

This dismissal was a pivotal moment in Oliver's fight for justice, as it highlighted the systemic barriers that protect institutions like Penn State from accountability. The "Pennsylvania

Corruption Machine" operates through a network of interlocking protections—administrators who violate university
policies, attorneys who misrepresent facts, and oversight
bodies like the Disciplinary Board that refuse to act, even when
the evidence is undeniable. These barriers create an environment where injustices can thrive without consequences.

For Oliver, an immigrant student who had already faced
discrimination, retaliation, and procedural violations, the
Board's decision was a crushing blow. It reinforced the reality
that the system is designed to protect the powerful, not the
vulnerable. This moment forced Oliver and her family [advo-
cates] to confront the harsh truth of their situation and the
challenges they faced.

The Board's decision also fueled our determination to
expose these injustices. We wanted to shine a light on the
mechanics of the "Pennsylvania corruption machine," highlighting the systemic flaws that allow these issues to persist.
Our goal is to demand reform for the countless students who
face similar battles in the shadows of higher education.

# CHAPTER 8

# A CASE STUDY IN
# SYSTEMIC FAILURE

It is important to understand Oliver's fight against the Pennsylvania corruption machine. Penn State's actions reflect a wider systemic failure in higher education. This includes the lack of accountability for administrators who violate university policies, particularly when their actions target students who challenge discriminatory practices.

Universities, be they private or public, often operate as self-regulating entities. They have internal safeguards and policies, which are intended to ensure fairness. However, these tools do not always work as intended; they are easily manipulated or ignored when the institution's interests are at stake. Certainly, the misuse of protection tools to harm students is a violation in itself. Therefore, for minority and immigrant students like Oliver, who may already face systemic barriers in academia, these violations are particularly devastating.

Minority students are less likely to have the resources, networks, or institutional knowledge to navigate these processes, which makes them straightforward targets for retaliation and procedural misconduct. The failure to enforce policies such as GCAC-803, combined with the lack of oversight for

administrators with conflicts of interest, creates an environment where students who speak out against discrimination are
silenced through unlawful dismissals. A system that prioritizes
institutional protection over justice can derail their academic
careers.

The systemic failures in Oliver's case extended beyond
higher education to the legal system, where oversight bodies
and legal representatives further protected Penn State from
accountability. As discussed earlier, their formal response to the
Pennsylvania Human Relations Commission (PHRC) was not
truthful. Penn State's attorneys from Buchanan Ingersoll &
Rooney PC, George Charles Morrison, Andrew Thomas
Simmons, and Keith Michael Lee, misrepresented a critical fact.
They claimed that Oliver "had not requested a grade adjudication prior to her January 31, 2024, academic dismissal letter."

This was a blatant falsehood, since Oliver's email from 24
January 2024 to multiple university offices, with an attached
document formalizing the request, directly contradicted the
university's claim. This misrepresentation violated Rule 3.3 of
the Pennsylvania Rules of Professional Conduct (Candor toward
the Tribunal), which requires lawyers to be truthful in their
representations to an administrative body such as the PHRC.
Such rules are fundamental to maintaining the integrity of the
legal process and ensuring fairness in proceedings.

The falsehood was not a mere oversight; it was a calculated
move to obscure the violation of due process and retaliation
that underpinned Oliver's dismissal. This action misled the
PHRC and tainted the investigation, clearly affecting the
outcomes for Oliver and others in similar situations. The consequences of such misrepresentation highlight significant flaws
in both the accountability mechanisms within higher education
and the legal protections intended to uphold fairness.

When Oliver filed complaints against attorneys with the

Disciplinary Board of the Supreme Court of Pennsylvania, she hoped for accountability. However, on October 8, 2024, the Board dismissed her complaints, asserting that they were unable to establish a violation of the Rules of Professional Conduct through a preponderance of the evidence. The Board's reasoning was baffling: the evidence of the attorneys' misrepresentation was irrefutable. They argued that it did not clearly violate a specific rule.

They further stated that the issues Oliver raised were matters of fact and law for the PHRC to determine, not the Disciplinary Board. This suggestion left Oliver frustrated and confused. The Board also proposed that she resubmit her complaint if the PHRC or a court made a specific finding of misconduct.

This dismissal created a catch-22: The PHRC might not have addressed the attorneys' misconduct if the Disciplinary Board did not act. In turn, the Board would not have acted without a finding from the PHRC. This circular reasoning ensured that the misrepresentation would go unpunished, which left Oliver to face the consequences of a tainted investigation without recourse.

The dismissal of the Disciplinary Board is a textbook example of systemic failure in the legal system, where oversight bodies tasked with ensuring ethical conduct by attorneys often prioritize procedural technicalities over justice. The Board's refusal to hold attorneys accountable, despite unmistakable evidence of their violation of Rule 3.3, reflects a broader pattern of institutional protection for powerful entities like Penn State and their well-connected legal representatives. The blurred lines between ethical conduct and procedural adherence highlight a significant problem within the system.

For students like this complainant, the lack of resources to navigate these complex systems makes this failure particularly devastating. These individuals are at a disadvantage, unable to effectively advocate for their rights or challenge powerful institutions. But the lack of accountability from the legal system only serves to exacerbate their situation.

The legal system, which should serve as a safeguard on institutional misconduct, instead becomes complicit in it; they allow universities to evade accountability through deceptive tactics and procedural loopholes. This compromise not only undermines trust in the legal and educational systems but also perpetuates a cycle of injustice that affects many. As long as these systemic failures remain unaddressed, those seeking justice will continue to face insurmountable barriers.

Oliver's story also highlights the disproportionate impact of these systemic failures on minority and immigrant students. As a doctoral student who had already faced discrimination, Oliver was particularly vulnerable to retaliation and procedural violations. Her status as a minority or immigrant student made her a target for the administrator's discriminatory act, and the subsequent retaliation; they dismissed her just 29 days after her discrimination complaint. Thereby, they exploited the complainant's lack of institutional power to harm her by the very institutions designed to protect her.

Oliver was unable to seek justice due to a combination of systemic barriers created by the university's actions, the attorneys' misrepresentation, and the Disciplinary Board's dismissal. This pattern is not unique to Oliver; it reflects a broader reality in higher education and the legal system, where vulnerable students are systematically silenced, their voices drowned out by the machinery of institutional protection.

The "Pennsylvania Corruption Machine," of which Oliver is a microcosm, represents systemic failures that extend far beyond Penn State. In higher education, universities often operate with impunity, violating their policies to protect their reputation and silence dissent. This culture of disregard for established procedures fosters an environment in which accountability is minimal.

In the legal system, oversight bodies like the Disciplinary Board fail to hold attorneys accountable even when their misconduct is undeniable. This lack of oversight creates a culture of impunity that encourages institutions to act without fear of consequences. As a result, both educational and legal institutions perpetuate injustices without repercussions.

For minority and immigrant students, these failures are particularly acute, as they face intersecting barriers of discrimination, retaliation, and procedural misconduct, with little recourse to fight back. Systemic problems place these students at a disadvantage, often leaving them vulnerable in academic and legal settings. Their challenges highlight the urgent need for advocacy and reform.

Oliver's story is a call to action; it is a demand for reform in higher education and the legal system. It underscores the need to enforce policies, hold administrators accountable, and discipline attorneys for misconduct. Most importantly, it advocates for vulnerable students to be protected, not punished, for speaking out against injustice.

# CHAPTER 9

# NOT A LEGITIMATE LEGAL RESPONSE

THE LETTER of the Disciplinary Board, dated October 8, 2024, is an illegitimate legal response in the context of Oliver's well-documented case. This is significant, given its role in setting the stage for the PHRC's finding a few weeks later that Penn State did nothing wrong. The implications of this response highlight a troubling trend in the handling of such complaints.

The Board failed to address a significant ethical violation when it dismissed Oliver's complaint against the attorneys, despite straightforward evidence of their misrepresentation. This failure not only undermined the integrity of the PHRC investigation but also contributed to a broader pattern of systemic protection for Penn State. Such actions raise concerns about the accountability of legal and ethical standards within the institution.

The board letter was not a legitimate legal response. Its flawed reasoning, its failure to uphold the Pennsylvania Rules of Professional Conduct (RPC), and its impact on the subsequent ruling are unequivocal. It is important to integrate this understanding into the broader context of the case. It is also pertinent to show how the Board's actions reflect systemic failures that enabled the PHRC findings.

## CORRUPTION AT WORK

The letter of the Disciplinary Board dismissing Oliver's complaints against the attorneys of Penn State, George Charles Morrison, Andrew Thomas Simmons, and Keith Michael Lee, was not a legitimate legal response. This partisan disposition made no sense for several reasons, notably legally, professionally, and [most importantly] ethically. Notwithstanding the potential favoritism due to the past professional/employment link between one of the attorneys and the court itself, and given the contemporaneous history between them as well, the board had a clear conflict of interest as to how it approached the complaint against a former affiliate of the Pennsylvania judicial system.

On his official personal biographical page on the Buchanan Ingersoll & Rooney PC website, attorney George C. Morrison claimed: "Prior to joining private practice, George was a judicial clerk to the Supreme Court of Pennsylvania and also served as a judicial clerk to the Commonwealth Court of Pennsylvania.' This reality implies that Morrison, one of the attorneys involved in the false statement, which, by all accounts, should constitute professional misconduct under the duty of candor to a tribunal rule, is deeply embedded in Pennsylvania's state judicial culture. Mr. Morrison likely has strong professional connections with judges who would sit in the review of the PHRC matter.

Even if not improper, Morrison's credibility and familiarity with court expectations may create institutional sympathy in his favor. The Board's decision to dismiss the case seems to be rooted in its failure to address clear evidence of misconduct, its questionable legal reasoning, and its role in allowing the PHRC's subsequent ruling in Penn State's favor. These considerations suggest that the PA Disciplinary Board was never an impartial arbitrator in the matter. The appearance of bias is inevitable, even in the absence of actual influence. A former clerk of Pennsylvania's highest courts possesses institutional familiarity and credibility that ordinary complainants, such as Oliver, lack.

*1. Failure to Address Clear Evidence of Misrepresentation*

The core issue in Oliver's complaints was the misrepresentation in their July 15, 2024, formal response to the PHRC on July 15, 2024, where they claimed that Oliver "had not requested a grade adjudication prior to her academic dismissal letter from the College of Nursing on January 31, 2024." This statement was demonstrably false, as Oliver had emailed a formal request for grade adjudication on January 24, 2024, to multiple university offices and university officials, including the administrator responsible for grade adjudication (who was also named in her January 2, 2024, discrimination complaint), the Grad Dean's Office, and others, with an attached document formalizing the request. This email, sent seven days before her dismissal, directly contradicted the attorneys' claim, making their statement a clear falsehood.

The Pennsylvania Rules of Professional Conduct (RPC), specifically Rule 3.3 (Candor Toward the Tribunal), explicitly require lawyers to be truthful in their representations to a tribunal or administrative body like the PHRC. For instance, rule 3.3(a)(1) states that a lawyer shall not knowingly "make a false statement of material fact or law to a tribunal or fail to correct a false statement of material fact or law previously made to the tribunal by the lawyer." The attorneys' claim was a false statement of material fact, as the existence of the grade adjudication request was central to Oliver's case: it demonstrated that Penn State dismissed her without addressing her pending request, which is a due process violation under the law. The email further supported Ms. Oliver's retaliation claim, given the close temporal proximity (29 days) between her discrimination complaint and her dismissal on January 31st dismissal.

The Disciplinary Board's letter acknowledged Oliver's complaint but dismissed it, claiming they could not "substantiate a violation of the RULES of Professional Conduct based upon [her] allegations." In a clever strategy, the Board treated the issue as if the attorneys had contested Ms. Oliver's argument in an adversarial setting. However, this is not what happened. Ms. Oliver did not make a statement that contradicts the attorney's position. She did not contest their position, as the Board implies that she did. In fact, only the opposite is true. Here, the attorneys made a statement that was demonstrably false, for which Ms. Oliver provided the appropriate evidence that the statement itself was incorrect.

The Board treated Ms. Oliver's rebuttal of the attorney's statement as the initial statement itself, which implied that the attorneys were the ones who rebutted her statement to defend their "client's interest," as the Board denotes. The Board argued that they could only discipline attorneys for conduct that "clearly violates a specific rule" and that any clear violation must be established by a "preponderance of the evidence." This reasoning is deeply flawed, considering the evidence presented. The email was not speculative. It clearly showed that the attorneys' statement was simply false.

The January 24, 2024, email was irrefutable proof of the attorneys' falsehood. It met the preponderance of the evidence standard, which requires only that the evidence indicates that it is more likely than not that the violation occurred. The email was not a matter of interpretation or ambiguity; it was a concrete record of Oliver's request. It directly contradicted the lawyer's claim, which was made independently and as a defense of a separate but also related claim in the formal PHRC complaint against the university. This email provides a clear and evident violation of professional conduct rules.

The Board's failure to recognize this as a clear violation of Rule 3.3 undermines the legitimacy of their response. It suggests either a willful disregard of the evidence or a misapplication of the legal standard. Such oversight raises concerns about accountability mechanisms within the Board and the integrity of the disciplinary process.

*2. Questionable Legal Reasoning and Circular Logic*

The reasoning further erodes the legitimacy of their response by relying on questionable legal arguments and circular logic. The Board stated that the issues raised by Oliver, specifically the validity of the attorney's statements to the PHRC, were "matters of fact and law" that could be determined by the PHRC, rather than by the Disciplinary Board. They suggested that if the PHRC or a court made a specific written finding of misconduct by the attorneys, Oliver could resubmit her complaint with that finding for further evaluation. This response created a catch-22 that effectively ensured that the misconduct would go unaddressed.

The Board's argument that the PHRC should determine the validity of the attorney's statements ignores the Board's own role in enforcing the RPC. The primary mandate is to investigate discrimination and retaliation, not to investigate attorney misconduct under the RPC. While the PHRC could consider the misrepresentation as part of its investigation, it is not a disciplinary body for attorneys; that role, arguably, only belongs to the Pennsylvania Disciplinary Board. In effect, the Board required Oliver to prove the very misconduct that the Board itself had the exclusive duty to investigate, a procedural catch-22 that guaranteed impunity.

By deferring to the PHRC, the Board abdicated its responsibility to enforce Rule 3.3, which exists precisely to ensure that attorneys do not mislead tribunals or administrative bodies through false statements. The Board's suggestion that Oliver wait for a PHRC finding of misconduct before resubmitting her complaint created a circular loop. This circular reasoning ensured that the misrepresentation would go unpunished, thereby leaving Oliver to face the consequences of a tainted investigation without recourse.

The implication of inaction by the Board undermines the integrity of the legal process. In this case, attorney misconduct leaves both the victim and the system vulnerable to its repercussions. Instead of fostering accountability, the board approach effectively protects attorneys from facing the consequences of their actions. They further complicated justice for those harmed. By failing to enforce its own ethical standards, the Board not only abdicated state responsibility but also created the conditions for federal concern, namely, that state institutions were willfully ignoring misrepresentation to protect a powerful university.

The Board's claim that the attorneys' misrepresentation did not "clearly violate a specific rule" is legally unsound. Rule 3.3 is a specific rule that addresses false representation during court proceedings, either in a tribunal or in any judicial setting. The false statement about the grade adjudication request was a clear violation of that rule.

The Board's claim of not being able to substantiate the violation through a preponderance of evidence is equally unsustainable given that the January 24 email presented clear and undisputed proof of the falsehood. The reasoning appears to be a pretext to avoid action. This legal maneuvering reflected a systemic reluctance to hold well-connected attorneys accountable, particularly when they represent a powerful institution like Penn State.

### 3. Enabling the PHRC's Finding Through Inaction

The dismissal of the Disciplinary Board on October 8, 2024, set the stage for the PHRC finding a few weeks later that Penn State did nothing wrong. In addition, they highlight the illegitimacy of the Board's response. The misrepresentation was a critical piece of the defense of Penn State before the PHRC.

By falsely claiming that Oliver had not requested a grade adjudication, the attorneys obscured the due process violation (dismissing Oliver without addressing her pending request) and the retaliation angle (the administrator's conflict of interest and the close temporal proximity between the discrimination complaint and dismissal). This misrepresentation tainted the investigation of the PHRC, as it allowed Penn State to present a distorted version of the facts. The conduct [itself] was detrimental to the complainant, thereby undermining Oliver's claims of discrimination and retaliation.

Had the Disciplinary Board acted on Oliver's complaints and found that the attorneys were in violation of Rule 3.3, it would have sent a clear signal to the PHRC that Penn State's defense was built on a foundation of deceit. This finding could have prompted the PHRC to scrutinize university actions more closely, particularly the noted procedural violations (lack of participation of the doctoral committee, failure to follow the required process, lack of advance notice, post-dismissal adjudication, and the leave of absence requirements) and retaliation evidence. Instead, the Board's dismissal effectively endorsed the misconduct of the attorneys, which allowed them to proceed without consequence and allowing the PHRC to rule in Penn State without addressing the misrepresentation.

The PHRC's finding that Penn State did nothing wrong

suggests that the Board's inaction, coming just weeks after its dismissal, had a major influence on the outcome of the investigation. The PHRC, lacking a disciplinary finding from the Board, may have accepted the attorney's false statement at face value or, at the very least, failed to attribute the misrepresentation of the weight it deserved in evaluating Penn State's actions. This outcome reflects a broader systemic failure: oversight bodies like the Disciplinary Board and the PHRC operate in silos, failing to coordinate their efforts to ensure justice and instead creating a system where misconduct goes unaddressed, and powerful institutions are protected through procedural loopholes and institutional bias.

*4. Reflecting Systemic Protection and the "Pennsylvania Corruption Machine"*

The letter from the Disciplinary Board was not a legitimate legal response because it reflects a broader pattern of systemic protection for Penn State. It is a reality described in the present context as the "Pennsylvania Corruption Machine," a term that is aptly echoed both here and elsewhere to describe the obstacles the family faced in their quest for justice in this matter. The Board's refusal to hold attorneys accountable, despite unambiguous evidence of their violation of Rule 3.3, mirrors the initial ruling in Penn State's favor (before the investigation was reopened) and the agency's final finding that the university did nothing wrong without a meaningful investigation and issuing the same flawed decision, which contains false information on Oliver's academic records. These decisions (taken together) suggest a systemic reluctance to challenge powerful institutions, even when their actions are unlawful and their representatives engage in misconduct.

A critical link in the chain of systemic failures designed to enable Penn State to avoid accountability was the Board's dismissal. By failing to address the misrepresentation of the attorneys, the Board allowed Penn State to present a distorted narrative to the PHRC, which undermined Oliver's claims of discrimination, retaliation, and procedural violations. The PHRC's subsequent finding that Penn State did nothing wrong was a direct consequence of this inaction, as it allowed the university to avoid scrutiny of policy violations (lack of doctoral committee involvement, failure to follow the required process, lack of advance notice), due process violations (ignoring the grade adjudication request, post-dismissal adjudication, the leave of absence requirement), and retaliation evidence (the administrator's conflict of interest, the 29-day gap between the discrimination complaint and dismissal, and the 7-day gap between the grade adjudication request and dismissal). The Board's letter, far from being a legitimate legal response, was a cog in the "Pennsylvania Corruption Machine," which was designed to ensure that Penn State's misconduct would go unpunished and that Oliver's fight for justice would be thwarted by a system designed to protect the powerful.

# CHAPTER 10

# SYSTEMIC FAILURES AND THE FINDING

THE ILLEGITIMATE RESPONSE had a direct impact on the findings a few weeks later. It reinforced the systemic failures in Oliver's case. The PHRC's ruling that Penn State did nothing wrong ignored the overwhelming evidence of misconduct: policy violations (the administrator's unilateral dismissal without doctoral committee involvement, failure to follow the required process ending with Dean and the lack of advance notice, as confirmed by the attorneys' statement); the due process violations (ignoring the grade adjudication request on January 24, 2024, conducting the adjudication post-dismissal, and imposing the Leave of Absence requirement); the retaliation evidence (the administrator's conflict of interest and the close temporal proximity); and the attorneys" misrepresentation (the false claim about the grade adjudication request). The Board's dismissal of the attorneys' misconduct allowed Penn State to present a sanitized version of events to the PHRC, free from the scrutiny that a disciplinary finding would have prompted.

This outcome reflects a broader pattern of systemic failures in higher education and the legal system, where universities and their representatives are protected through a combination of procedural violations, deceptive tactics, and institutional bias. For minority and immigrant students like Oliver, these failures are particularly acute, as they face intersecting barriers of discrimination, retaliation, and procedural misconduct, with little recourse to fight back. The letter of the Disciplinary Board critically enabled this systemic protection by failing to address the misrepresentation of the attorneys. It set the stage for the PHRC findings and ensured that Penn State would not face consequences for its actions.

The Board's decision was not a legitimate legal response because it failed to uphold the ethical standards of the legal profession, ignored unmistakable evidence of misconduct, and contributed to a broader institutional protection that allowed Penn State to evade accountability. It was a textbook example of the "Pennsylvania Corruption Machine" at work, where oversight bodies prioritize procedural technicalities over justice, thereby leaving vulnerable students like Oliver to bear the consequences of a system designed to protect the powerful.

## IMPLICATIONS

The Disciplinary Board's letter failed to address the attorneys' clear violation of Rule 3.3. It relied on questionable legal reasoning and circular logic. It enabled the PHRC to determine that Penn State did nothing wrong. The situation presents a combination of procedural violations, deceptive tactics, and institutional bias.

Although the inaction set the stage for the PHRC's ruling, it also drove home the importance of transparency and accountability within legal frameworks. The decision shows a broader narrative of systemic failures. It highlights how the Board's dismissal was a pivotal moment that extends far beyond the immediate situation, which revealed deep-rooted issues within institutional frameworks.

The decision can also serve as a call to action. It emphasizes that there must be reform in both higher education and the legal system. Such reforms are critical for making sure that oversight bodies like the Disciplinary Board and the PHRC fulfill their mandates. To truly protect vulnerable students from discrimination, retaliation, and procedural misconduct, we must empower these bodies to hold institutions and their representatives accountable.

Only through meaningful changes can we ensure that similar failures do not occur in the future. It is essential to create a safe environment in educational institutions where students feel safe in reporting misconduct. The current system must evolve to prioritize the well-being and rights of students over institutional interests.

# CHAPTER II

# DISMISSIVE TONE, CONDESCENDING LANGUAGE

It is important to discuss the dismissive tone, condescending language, and the adversarial nature of the Disciplinary Board's response in its letter of 8 October 2024 to Oliver. These elements further undermine the legitimacy of the Board's response and reinforce systemic failures in her case. This reality is particularly significant because it sets the stage for the PHRC to determine a few weeks later, that Penn State did nothing wrong.

These aspects of the letter offer important information about the modus operandi of the Pennsylvania corruption machine. The dismissive language of the correspondence highlights specific instances where the Board revealed its mindset and its attitude toward Oliver, the complainant. The letter did not solely reveal a dismissive tone, condescending language, and adversarial nature but also demonstrated how the machine operates, which is a layered approach whereby one institution sets the groundwork for the other to use as a legitimate framework to act later. This approach provides a much-needed veneer of institutional independence, where, in fact, it is the opposite. There is a clear interdependence in their conduct.

There is a need to develop a deeper understanding of the board's communication style. By examining these specific elements, the goal is to illustrate the broader implications that their actions had on the case. It is also vital to relay the impact the board letter had on the perception of fairness in the complaint process.

Examining the dismissive tone will help us decipher the broader implications of their decision in the context of the actions the PHRC later took against Oliver. The conduct shows how these elements reflect systemic bias and institutional protection. It is crucial to understand how such attitudes can alter the entire adjudicative process. Investigating these issues reveals that Oliver's environment was not conducive to achieving justice.

## ANALYSIS OF THE TONE AND LANGUAGE

The letter from the Disciplinary Board, although ostensibly a formal legal response, is laced with a dismissive tone, condescending language, and an adversarial stance that belittles Oliver's legitimate concerns and positions the Board as an opponent rather than an impartial oversight governmental body. These elements are evident throughout the letter and contribute to the perception that the Board's response was not a legitimate legal response but rather a reflection of systemic bias designed to protect Penn State and its attorneys.

*1. Dismissive Tone*

The dismissive tone of the letter is apparent in how the Board minimizes Oliver's complaints and fails to engage with the substance of her allegations. Specific examples include

**Minimizing the Misrepresentation**: The Board acknowledges Oliver's complaint about the misrepresentation of the attorneys, which claimed that they falsely claimed she had not requested a grade adjudication prior to her January 31, 2024, dismissal, but dismisses the complaint without addressing the evidence presented. The letter states: "While we appreciate your frustration as you have described it, because we cannot substantiate a violation of the RULES of Professional Conduct based on your allegations, we have dismissed the complaints." This statement is dismissive because it reduces Oliver's complaint to mere frustration rather than a serious allegation of ethical misconduct supported by straightforward evidence (January 24, 2024, email). The failure to engage with the email, which directly contradicts the attorney's claim, suggests a lack of thoughtful consideration, as if Oliver's complaint were an inconvenience rather than a legitimate grievance.

**Deferral to the PHRC**: The repeated assertion that the issues Oliver raised are "fact and law" for the PHRC to determine—"The issues you raise regarding the validity of facts or positions asserted by attorneys... are more appropriate for that tribunal to consider and determine"—is dismissive because it sidesteps the Board's own responsibility to enforce the Pennsylvania Rules of Professional Conduct (RPC). The attorneys' misrepresentation was a clear violation of Rule 3.3 (Candor Toward the Tribunal), which falls squarely within the Board's jurisdiction. The Board dismisses its role in addressing attorney misconduct by deferring to the PHRC, thereby avoiding the ethical implications of attorney actions.

**Catch-22 Suggestion**: The Board's suggestion that Oliver resubmit her complaint if the PHRC or a court makes a specific misconduct finding—'If in the course of the litigation there is a specific written finding made by the PHRC or a court that any of the attorneys committed misconduct... you can contact this office at that time'—is dismissive because it creates a circular loop that ensures that the attorneys' misconduct will go unaddressed. This response implies that Oliver's current complaint is not worthy of sincere consideration, shifting the burden back to her to obtain a finding from another body, despite the unmistakable evidence she has already provided.

The dismissive tone throughout the letter conveys a lack of empathy for Oliver's situation and a reluctance to engage in the substance of her allegations, treating her complaint as a procedural nuisance rather than a serious ethical violation that warrants investigation and action.

*2. Condescending Language*

The letter's language is condescending in its repeated explanations of the Board's role and limitations, as well as its assumptions about Oliver's understanding of the legal process. Specific examples include

**Overexplaining Basic Concepts: The** lengthy explanation of its jurisdiction and the scope of the RPC: First, you should know that this office has some limits on disciplinary complaints. Our jurisdiction and authority are limited to attempting to enforce the Rules of Professional Conduct, a set of minimum ethical standards with which all attorneys must abide. This decision is condescending because it assumes that Oliver lacks a basic understanding of the disciplinary process. Although some explanation may be necessary, the tone and repetition ('It is important for you to know," "the rules are quite broad in their scope; they simply do not prohibit all conduct") suggest that the Board views Oliver as naive or uninformed, rather than as a complainant with a legitimate grievance supported by evidence.

**Patronizing Dismissal of Her Role:** The Board's statement of the complaint was laden with bias. The noted: "Moreover, even though you have submitted complaints, this office does not represent you or your personal interests in PHRC matters." This was an indictment of the attorneys misconduct. They further noted: "We are not your attorney and cannot provide you with any personal legal advice." This language was dismissive and condescending. But this reflection unnecessarily demonstrated a point that Oliver already understands. As a doctoral student navigating a complex legal process, Oliver was clearly aware that the Board was not her attorney; her complaint was not a request for legal representation but a demand for accountability for the misconduct of the attorneys. The Board's emphasis on this point seems patronizing, as if it's necessary to remind Oliver of her role in the process.

**Implying Her Concerns Are Misplaced:** The Board's assertion that "the attorneys have a duty to pursue their client's interests, which may naturally oppose your interests," and that they "are not obligated to act at your direction or in accordance with your demands," is condescending because it implies that Oliver's complaint stems from a misunderstanding of the adversarial nature of legal proceedings. This frame ignores the substance of her allegation: that the attorneys' misrepresentation was not a legitimate defense tactic but a violation of ethical rules. By suggesting that Oliver's expectations are unreasonable, the Board diminishes the validity of her complaint, treating her as if she is overreacting to standard legal practice rather than raising a serious ethical concern.

The condescending language in the letter positions Oliver as an outsider who does not understand the legal system, rather than a complainant with a well-documented grievance. This tone reinforces the power imbalance between Oliver, a minority or immigrant student, and the institutional actors (the Board, the attorneys, and Penn State) who hold the authority in this process.

*3. Adversarial nature of the Response*

The adversarial nature is evident in how the Board positions itself as an opponent to Oliver. The board defended the attorneys and Penn State rather than acting as an impartial overseer of ethical conduct. Specific examples include

**Defending Attorneys' Actions**: The Board's statement that "the attorneys have a duty to pursue their client's interests, which may naturally oppose your interests," and that they "are not obligated to act at your direction or in accordance with your demands," is adversarial; it frames the attorneys' actions as legitimate advocacy, which ignores the ethical violation at the heart of Oliver's complaint. The misrepresentation was not a mere defense of the interest of Penn State. It was a false statement of material fact, which is in violation of Rule 3.3. By focusing on the duties of the attorneys to their client rather than their duties to the tribunal, the Board takes an adversarial stance, aligning itself with the attorneys and Penn State instead of addressing the ethical breach.

**Shifting the Burden Back to Oliver**: The Board's suggestion that Oliver consult with counsel. "If you have ongoing concerns, you should consult with counsel of your choosing who can advise you as to any potential rights, remedies, and options you may have"—and resubmit her complaint if the PHRC makes a finding of misconduct, which is adversarial because it places the burden back on Oliver to navigate a complex legal system, despite the Board's failure to act on clear evidence. This response portrays the PA Disciplinary Board as an adversary, unwilling to provide assistance or conduct an investigation, and instead forces Oliver to confront a system that has already let her down.

**Protecting the Confidentiality of Attorneys:** The Board's closing statement, "With few exceptions, unless the Office of Disciplinary Counsel files formal charges, the disciplinary matter remains confidential, and the respondent-attorney is not required to answer to the complainant," is adversarial; it prioritizes the attorneys' protection over Oliver's right to accountability. This statement ensures that attorneys face no immediate consequences for their misconduct, shielding them from scrutiny while leaving Oliver without recourse. The emphasis on confidentiality and the attorneys' lack of obligation to answer to them reinforces an adversarial dynamic, where the system protects the attorneys and Penn State at Oliver's expense.

The adversarial nature of the response positions the Board as a defender of the status quo; they seemed more concerned with protecting the attorneys and Penn State than with ensuring ethical conduct. This position undermines the Board's role as an impartial overseer and contributes to the perception that its response was not a legitimate legal response but a reflection of systemic bias.

## INTEGRATION WITH A WIDER CONTEXT: SYSTEMIC FAILURES AND THE FINDING

The dismissive tone, condescending language, and adversarial nature of the Disciplinary Board letter are not just stylistic flaws; they are indicative of deeper systemic failures that enabled the PHRC to conclude a few weeks later that Penn State did nothing wrong. These elements reflect a broader pattern of institutional protection: the "Pennsylvania Corruption Machine," where oversight bodies prioritize procedural technicalities and institutional interests over justice, particularly for vulnerable students like Oliver.

*1. Reinforcing systemic bias and the "Pennsylvania Corruption Machine"*

The dismissive tone, condescending language, and adversarial stance reflect a systemic bias that protects powerful institutions such as Penn State and their representatives. The failure to engage with the evidence of attorney misrepresentation (the

January 24, 2024) and its deferral to the PHRC suggest a reluctance to challenge Penn State, even when the evidence of misconduct is clear. This reluctance mirrors the initial ruling in Penn State's favor (before the investigation was reopened) and their final finding that the university did nothing wrong, despite overwhelming evidence of participation in the policy violations (lack of doctoral committee, failure to follow the required process, lack of advance notice), due process violations (ignoring the grade adjudication request, post-dismissal adjudication, the leave of absence requirement), and retaliation (administrator conflict of interest, the 29-day gap between the discrimination complaint and dismissal, and the 7-day gap between the grade adjudication request and dismissal).

The tone and language of the Board's letter reinforce this systemic bias by treating Oliver as an outsider who does not understand the legal system, rather than a complainant with a legitimate complaint. This dynamic is particularly acute for minority and immigrant students like Oliver, who face intersecting barriers of discrimination, retaliation, and procedural misconduct. The adversarial stance—defending the Board, defending the attorneys' actions, shifting the burden back to Oliver, and protecting the confidentiality of the attorneys—ensures that the system continues to stack up against her, which allowed Penn State to evade accountability through a combination of deceptive tactics and institutional protection.

*2. Setting the stage for the PHRC's Finding*

The Board's dismissive, condescending, and adversarial response set the stage for the PHRC finding a few weeks later that Penn State did nothing wrong by failing to address the attorneys' misrepresentation, which was a critical piece of Penn State's defense. The incorrect statement that Oliver didn't ask for a grade review hid the violation of her rights (not considering her request before dismissing her) and the issue of retaliation (the administrator's conflict of interest and the timing), which affected the PHRC's investigation. The Board's refusal to find the attorneys in violation of Rule 3.3 allowed Penn State to present a distorted narrative to the PHRC, which was free from the scrutiny that a disciplinary finding would have prompted.

The ruling of the PHRC, coming shortly after the Board's dismissal, suggests that the Board's inaction had an important influence on the outcome. The PHRC, lacking a disciplinary finding from the Board, may have accepted the attorney's false statement at face value or, at the very least, failed to give the misrepresentation of the weight it deserved in evaluating Penn State's actions. The dismissive tone and adversarial stance of the Board signaled to the PHRC that Oliver's complaint was not serious. It reinforced the narrative that her allegations were unfounded, which led to the presumption that the university did nothing wrong.

This outcome reflects a broader systemic failure: oversight bodies like the Disciplinary Board and the PHRC operate in silos by failing to coordinate their efforts to ensure justice. Instead, they created a system where misconduct goes unaddressed and powerful institutions are protected through procedural loopholes and institutional bias.

3. *Impact on Vulnerable Students*

The tone and language are particularly harmful in the context of Oliver's status as a minority or immigrant student. The dismissive and condescending approach—reducing her complaint to "frustration," over-explaining basic concepts, and implying her concerns are misplaced—exacerbates the power imbalance between Oliver and the institutional actors (the Board, the attorneys, and Penn State). This kind of communication creates an environment that is unwelcoming and hostile to Oliver and others in similar positions.

The response takes an adversarial stance, portraying the

Board as an adversary instead of an unbiased supervisor. They further isolated Oliver. This dynamic demonstrates that the system's purpose is not to uphold it, but rather to safeguard those in authority. Such an environment can deeply affect the confidence and willingness to engage with the institution that is meant to serve them.

For vulnerable students, who may already face systemic barriers in academia and the legal system, this treatment is particularly devastating. It reinforces their marginalization and discourages them from seeking justice. This kind of response can perpetuate a cycle of silence and inaction within marginalized groups. They further entrench existing inequalities.


## A REFLECTION OF SYSTEMIC FAILURES

The letter of the Disciplinary Board was not a legitimate legal response, not only because of its failure to address the clear violation of Rule 3.3 and its questionable legal reasoning, but also because of its dismissive tone, condescending language, and adversarial nature. These elements reflect a systemic bias that prioritizes institutional protection over justice, particularly for vulnerable students like Oliver. The Board's response set the stage for the PHRC's finding a few weeks later that Penn State did nothing wrong by failing to address the misrepresentation of the attorneys, which allowed Penn State to present a distorted narrative and evade accountability for its misconduct.

The dismissive tone, condescending language, and adversarial stance are indicative of the "Pennsylvania Corruption Machine" at work—a system where oversight bodies like the Disciplinary Board and the PHRC protect powerful institutions through procedural technicalities, institutional bias, and lack of accountability. For Oliver, a minority or immigrant student who faced discrimination, retaliation, and procedural violations, the

Board's response was a crushing blow. It reinforced the reality that the system is designed to protect the powerful, not the vulnerable. Oliver's poignant story is a call to action, which demands reform in higher education and the legal system to ensure that oversight bodies fulfill their mandates, hold institutions and their representatives accountable, and protect students from the systemic failures that the Board's letter so starkly exemplifies.

# CHAPTER 12

# ANALYSIS IN THE CONTEXT OF THE CASE

THE LETTER of the Disciplinary Board dismisses Oliver's complaints against the attorneys (George Charles Morrison, Andrew Thomas Simmons, and Keith Michael Lee) of Buchanan Ingersoll & Rooney PC, who represent Penn State in the PHRC matter. The dismissal is based on the Board's determination that the attorneys' actions, specifically their misrepresentation in the July 15, 2024, formal response to the PHRC, do not constitute a clear violation of the Pennsylvania Rules of Professional Conduct (RPC) by a preponderance of the evidence.

In this response, the attorneys claimed that Oliver had not requested a grade adjudication prior to her January 31, 2024, dismissal. This misrepresentation was a point of contention for Oliver. It is important to consider the implications of such claims in legal settings and the standards that govern the behavior of the attorney.

There is a need to analyze this in the context of the case. Understanding the relationship between the dismissal of Oliver's complaints and the conduct of the attorneys can help clarify the procedural safeguards in place. This analysis might also shed light on how such determinations impact the parties involved.


## THE REASONING OF THE DISCIPLINARY BOARD

The Board argues that its jurisdiction is limited to enforcing the Rules of Professional Conduct, which set minimum ethical standards for attorneys. They state that not all "unprofessional" or "unethical" conduct violates these rules, and they can only discipline attorneys for conduct that clearly violates a specific rule.

They assert that they cannot substantiate a violation of the RPC based on Oliver's allegations, despite unambiguous evidence of misrepresentation (the email on January 24, 2024, proves that Oliver requested a grade adjudication, contrary to the claim of the attorneys).

The Board emphasizes that they do not represent Oliver, cannot provide legal advice, and cannot intervene in the PHRC proceedings. They argue that the issues Oliver raises (the validity of the attorney's statements to the PHRC) are matters of fact and law for the PHRC to determine, not the Disciplinary Board.

They suggest that if the PHRC or a court makes a specific written finding of misconduct by the attorneys, Oliver can resubmit her complaint with that finding for further evaluation. This process allows for a reassessment of her case based on new evidence of misconduct. It ensures that any clear wrongdoing by attorneys is considered, which could affect the outcome of her complaint.

The presumption here is that submitting a revised complaint can provide Oliver with a clearer path to address her grievances. If the attorneys involved acknowledge their misconduct, this action could result in taking appropriate measures against them. Therefore, the findings not only serve as a basis for resubmission but also signify the importance of accountability in legal practice.

## IMPLICATIONS FOR ATTORNEY MISREPRESENTATION

The misrepresentation in their July 15, 2024, response to the PHRC that Oliver had not requested a grade adjudication prior to her dismissal is a clear falsehood, as evidenced by her January 24, 2024, email. This misrepresentation violates Rule 3.3 of the Pennsylvania Rules of Professional Conduct (Candor toward the Tribunal), which requires lawyers to be truthful in their representations to a tribunal or administrative body such as the PHRC.

The dismissal of the complaint, despite this unmistakable evidence, suggests a reluctance to hold attorneys accountable, supporting the argument about the "Pennsylvania Corruption Machine" and systemic protection for Penn State and its representatives. The Board's reasoning, that the misrepresentation does not clearly violate the RPC by a preponderance of evidence, is questionable, as the evidence (the January 24 email) directly contradicts the attorneys' claim, making the falsehood undeniable.

## REINFORCING THE NARRATIVE OF "PENNSYLVANIA CORRUPTION MACHINE"

The dismissal of the complaint, despite straightforward evidence of misrepresentation, reinforces the narrative that Penn State has relied on systemic protection to avoid accountability. The Board's refusal to act on attorneys' misconduct mirrors the initial ruling in Penn State's favor, despite the discrimination complaint, due process violations, and policy violations (lack of participation in the notice, lack of a doctoral committee, failure to follow the process, post-dismissal adjudication, and the absence requirement).

The Board's suggestion that Oliver wait for a specific finding of misconduct from the PHRC or a court before submitting her complaint creates a catch-22: the PHRC may not address the misconduct if the Disciplinary Board does not act, and the Board will not act without a finding from the PHRC. This circular reasoning further supports the argument that the system is designed to protect powerful institutions such as Penn State, which allowed them to evade accountability through procedural loopholes.

## IMPLICATIONS FOR THE PHRC INVESTIGATION

The dismissal of the Disciplinary Board shifts the burden back to the PHRC to address the misrepresentation as part of their reopened investigation. The PHRC must now consider not only the discrimination and retaliation allegations but also the procedural violations, and the misconduct of the misrepresentation directly affects the integrity of the investigation.

If the PHRC rules in Penn State's favor without addressing the misrepresentation, it would further support the argument that the decision was made "by force," as part of the "Pennsylvania Corruption Machine." The misrepresentation obscures the due process violation (dismissing Oliver without addressing her grade adjudication request) and the retaliation angle (the administrator's conflict of interest and the close temporal proximity between the discrimination complaint and the dismissal of 31 people), which makes it critical for the PHRC to address this problem.

## PUBLIC ACCOUNTABILITY AND ADVOCACY

The dismissal of the Disciplinary Board, despite the unmistakable evidence of misrepresentation, provides additional evidence for public advocacy efforts. It highlights the systemic protection that Penn State and its attorneys have received, even when their misconduct is undeniable. The book and public posts can use this evidence to frame Oliver's case as a textbook example of systemic failure in higher education and the legal system, particularly in the context of discrimination and retaliation against minority or immigrant students.

The board dismissal can be presented as a failure of oversight. It reinforced the call for public scrutiny and reform. If the PHRC also fails to address the misrepresentation, it would be a clear example of a "decision by force," amplifying the narrative about the "Pennsylvania Corruption Machine."

## CONCLUSION AND RECOMMENDATIONS

The letter from the Disciplinary Board, dated October 8, 2024, dismisses Oliver's complaints against the attorneys, despite unambiguous evidence of misrepresentation in their July 15, 2024, response to the PHRC. The Board's argument that the misrepresentation does not clearly breach the Rules of Professional Conduct based on a preponderance of evidence is questionable. This dismissal reinforces the narrative of the "Pennsylvania Corruption Machine," as it suggests systemic protection for Penn State and its representatives, even when their misconduct is evident.

The January 24, 2024, email directly contradicts the attorneys' claim, which makes the falsehood undeniable. This contradiction raises concerns about the integrity of the attorneys and the overall judicial process in this case. The situation calls into question not only the actions of those involved but also the mechanisms in place to uphold accountability within the legal system.

The dismissal shifts the burden to the PHRC to address the misrepresentation of attorneys, along with discrimination, retaliation, and procedural violations (lack of involvement in the notice, lack of a doctoral committee, failure to follow the process, post-dismissal adjudication, and the leave of absence requirement). These issues highlight significant concerns about the integrity of the process and the fairness of the results. It is crucial that the PHRC take these matters seriously to maintain justice and accountability.

If the PHRC rules in Penn State's favor without addressing these issues, it would support the argument that the decision was made "by force," as part of the "Pennsylvania Corruption Machine." This could have far-reaching implications not only for the individuals involved but also for the reputation of the institution. Perception of corruption can undermine trust and lead to a greater questioning of institutional practices.

By memorializing the case in the public record through the book and posts, the strategy effectively holds Penn State accountable. Public documentation can act as a potent advocacy tool, amplifying the voices of those harmed. Especially if the dismissal of the Disciplinary Board and the attorneys' misconduct resonate with broader issues of systemic fairness and equity, this approach can foster greater awareness and drive necessary changes.

**Highlighting the dismissal of the disciplinary board.** The disciplinary board convened with great anticipation. The goal was to fulfil its purpose of upholding standards and ensuring accountability. However, as discussed in this section, this was not the case in this instance. By refusing to address the attorneys" misconduct, it became increasingly evident that the board's authority was being called into question.

Oliver expressed concerns over procedural fairness and the integrity of the process, which led to a heated debate about the board's legitimacy and impartiality. It is important to emphasize the dismissal of the complaint, despite the unambiguous evidence of misrepresentation, as evidence of systemic protection for Penn State. This dismissal raises significant questions about the integrity of the oversight processes in place.

The January 24, 2024 correspondence is a critical piece of evidence. This email emerged as undeniable proof of misrepresentation within an academic institution. The contents of the email meticulously outlined the discrepancies and inaccuracies that had been overlooked. It also drew attention to the Disciplinary Board's decision, which revealed a troubling lapse in oversight.

This failure was not merely an isolated incident; it became a part of a larger narrative that had been circulating regarding the "Pennsylvania Corruption Machine." This narrative hinted at systemic issues deeply rooted within the institution, which suggests that the circumstances surrounding the dismissal were indicative of broader problems that warranted scrutiny and reflection. As the evidence piled up in this case, it became increasingly clear that the challenges faced were not just a matter of individual accountability but were reflective of deeper, institutional shortcomings and the desire of oversight institutions to cover up the wrongdoing.

The implications of this dismissal are significant. It not only erodes the accountability that should be present in such disciplinary actions, but it also fosters a culture of protectionism for those involved. Such actions further fuel the perception of a systemic issue that goes beyond individual cases. They point to a larger problem within the governance of Penn State university.

The misrepresentation in Oliver's case was not merely a standalone issue; it intertwined with other grave violations that highlighted the failures of due process and retaliation. As Oliver's appeal regarding her grade adjudication went ignored, her dismissal took on a troubling dimension, which seemingly overshadowed by the administrator's inherent conflict of interest.

The close temporal proximity between Oliver's appeal and the subsequent dismissal raised further questions about the motives behind the actions taken against her. Together, these elements not only obscured the critical due process violation but also cast doubt on the legitimacy of Oliver's dismissal. They revealed a web of misconduct that could not easily be untangled.

**A Case of Systemic Failure**: The dismissal of the Disciplinary Board showcased a profound systemic failure within both higher education and the legal system. It reveals how powerful institutions frequently prioritize their own interests over the pursuit of justice. In Oliver's case, this neglect left her vulnerable to the very misconduct that the systems were designed to combat. The incident underscored the urgent need for accountability within these frameworks, as the lack thereof not only failed to protect victims like Oliver but also deprived them of fair treatment within an environment that should have shielded them from such injustices.

In a world where powerful institutions and their representatives often find themselves shielded from accountability, even in the face of evident misconduct, the need for reform becomes increasingly undeniable. As the inherent flaws within the system come to light, they spark conversations about the urgent need for change. This growing awareness resonates not only with the general public but also with advocacy groups, underscoring the critical importance of addressing these pervasive issues.

Oliver's situation highlighted the pressing need for transparency and reform within higher education and legal institutions. As the story unfolded, it became clear that the ramifications of systemic failures could no longer be ignored. This narrative served as a powerful illustration of how abuse of power flourished in such environments, which may prompt a broader discussion about the necessity for better safeguards. In turn, this focus on Oliver's experience not only deepened the impact of the book but also opened a vital platform for dialogue and potential change.

**PHRC's Final Ruling:** The PHRC ruled in favor of Penn State, prompting the need to examine various elements of the case, including the dismissal of the Disciplinary Board, the misrepresentation by attorneys, and other violations. These factors could be woven into an argument that the decision was coerced, which is indicative of a broader issue within what referred here to as the "Pennsylvania Corruption Machine." This narrative highlighted the systemic flaws at play. The goal is to rally support to challenge the outcome.

The PHRC's decision came as a disappointment, as it did not rule in Oliver's favor. Had the ruling been different, it could have marked a significant legal victory, which would have provided a powerful highlight for advocacy efforts aimed at fostering systemic reform. Instead of strengthening the call for change and serving as an inspiring example for those in search of justice, the outcome fell short of galvanizing the momentum needed to elevate public awareness about the urgent need for modifications within the system.

# PART FOUR
# APPELLATE BRIEF

## A STRATEGIC APPEAL TO THE DISCIPLINARY BOARD OF THE SUPREME COURT OF PENNSYLVANIA

OLIVER-JOHNSON VS PENNSYLVANIA
[FOR THE RECORD]

CHAPTER 13

# APPELLATE BRIEF
# (LIGHTLY EDITED)

## II. JURISDICTIONAL STATEMENT

THE SUPREME COURT of Pennsylvania has jurisdiction over this matter pursuant to Article V, Section 2 of the Pennsylvania Constitution and Pa.R.A.P. 1511, which grants the Court the authority to review the decisions of the Disciplinary Board of the Supreme Court of Pennsylvania. This petition is timely filed within the 30-day period allowed by Pa.R.A.P. 1512(a)(1) following the Disciplinary Board's decision issued on June 1, 2024.[1] This case involves questions of procedural due process and substantive fairness, which makes it suitable for review by this Court.

The Petitioner, Oliver-Johnson,[2] seeks review of the Disciplinary Board's decision that failed to consider the evidence presented and resulted in denial of due process rights. The

---

1. This is a fictional date. The initial appeal was filed around November 2024.
2. This is a fictional name, which based on real names (Germine Oliver and Benjamin Johnson).

review sought is within the Court's jurisdiction as it involves questions of procedural due process and substantive fairness under Pennsylvania law.

## III. INTRODUCTION AND STATEMENT OF ISSUES

I am Oliver-Johnson, the Petitioner-Appellant in this case, seeking justice under the jurisdiction of the Supreme Court of Pennsylvania. I have pursued my rights within the legal framework of the Commonwealth, asserting that the attorneys involved in my case before the Pennsylvania Human Relations Commission (PHRC) violated their professional and ethical obligations. Despite presenting clear and documented evidence of false statements and misrepresentations made by these attorneys, the Disciplinary Board of the Supreme Court of Pennsylvania dismissed my complaint on June 1, 2024, claiming that their conduct fell within acceptable advocacy for their client.

The attorneys' actions include knowingly making false statements, in violation of Rule 8.4(c) of the Pennsylvania Rules of Professional Conduct, which prohibits dishonesty, fraud, deceit, or misrepresentation. Their actions further undermine Rule 8.4(d), which prohibits conduct prejudicial to the administration of justice. The Board's decision to dismiss my complaint without thorough investigation raises significant concerns about due process, transparency, and fairness.

The issues I present for review are:

1. Whether the Disciplinary Board erred by dismissing my complaint without a substantive examination of the evidence provided, in violation of due process as outlined in the Pennsylvania Constitution and relevant procedural rules.

2. Whether the Board's decision effectively allows attorneys to make false statements under the guise of client advocacy, contravening Rule 8.4(c) and 8.4(d) of the Pennsylvania Rules of Professional Conduct.

3. Whether the Board's handling of my case, including the use of dismissive language and lack of transparency, constituted a denial of my due process rights.

## IV. STATEMENT OF THE CASE

### A. Relevant Legal and Procedural Framework

Under Pennsylvania law, attorneys are held to strict ethical and professional standards to ensure the integrity of the legal process and protect the rights of all parties involved. These standards are codified in the Pennsylvania Rules of Professional Conduct, which outline the ethical obligations of attorneys to uphold honesty, integrity, and fairness in all legal proceedings.

Rule 8.4(c) explicitly prohibits attorneys from engaging in conduct involving dishonesty, fraud, deceit, or misrepresentation. This rule serves to maintain public trust in the legal profession and ensure that legal processes are not compromised by false or misleading statements. Rule 8.4(d) prohibits conduct that is prejudicial to the administration of justice. It reinforced the duty of legal professionals to act in ways that promote fairness and transparency in all judicial and administrative proceedings.

The Disciplinary Board of the Supreme Court of Pennsylvania is tasked with investigating and adjudicating complaints of professional misconduct against attorneys, as authorized by the Pennsylvania Constitution and relevant procedural rules.

These responsibilities include assessing whether attorneys have violated ethical obligations and determining appropriate sanctions where necessary.

In this case, I, Oliver-Johnson, sought relief through the Disciplinary Board by presenting documented evidence of misrepresentations made by attorneys representing the respondent in my case before the Pennsylvania Human Relations Commission (PHRC). The evidence included verifiable documentation that contradicted statements made by the attorneys, raising significant concerns about violations of Rule 8.4(c) and 8.4(d).

Despite the strength of the evidence provided, the Disciplinary Board issued a decision on June 1, 2024, dismissing my complaint and suggesting that the attorneys' actions were within the acceptable bounds of advocacy for their client. This decision raises critical questions regarding procedural due process, the administration of justice, and the integrity of disciplinary oversight within the state.

*B. Factual Background*

I am an accomplished professional in nursing with extensive experience in Medical Surgery, Intermediate Intensive Care Unit (IICU), Dialysis, Health Administration, and Nurse Education. I have been living in the United States since 1996. My journey in the nursing profession began in 2002, after completing my studies at New York Technical College. Over the years, I integrated into American society, built a reputable career, and raised my family in Pennsylvania.

In January 2024, I was a nursing student at Pennsylvania State University, completing a graduate degree in Doctor of Nursing Practice (DNP). I faced numerous academic and administrative obstacles, which led to my unexpected dismissal from the program. This action prompted me to file formal complaints, as I believed that the university's actions were discriminatory and retaliatory. The university's legal team submitted responses to the Pennsylvania Human Relations Commission (PHRC) that contained false and misleading claims regarding the timeline and nature of my academic progress and my requests for grade adjudication.

In the formal complaint filed by the PHRC, I noted the following: "On February 7, 2024, the school agreed to place the dismissal on hold and to allow the grade adjudication to occur post facto. However, the school placed me on a leave of absence." This entry prompted the following response from the university via the attorneys referenced in this appeal:

"Denied as stated. On February 7, 2024, Respondent informed Complainant that it would conduct a grade adjudication, even though Complainant had not requested a grade adjudication prior to her January 31, 2024, academic dismissal letter from the College of Nursing. By way of further response, Respondent informed Complainant that, pursuant to Penn State policy, she could request a Leave of Absence in order to maintain access to her Penn State email account and other amenities because Complainant had not registered for any classes for the Spring 2024 semester at that time."

In my complaint to the Disciplinary Board of the Supreme Court of Pennsylvania, I provided evidence showing that a formal request for grade adjudication was submitted on January 24, 2024, countering the attorneys' assertion that no such request was made before the dismissal on January 31, 2024. The attorneys also claimed that I had not completed two required courses, a statement refuted by official university records and correspondence, which confirmed that I had met my academic obligations prior to my dismissal.

Despite presenting this evidence, the Disciplinary Board of

the Supreme Court of Pennsylvania, in its decision dated June 1, 2024, chose to dismiss the complaint. The Board concluded that the attorneys' conduct fell within permissible advocacy aimed at protecting their client's interests, despite evidence pointing to clear violations of Rule 8.4(c), which prohibits dishonesty and misrepresentation, and Rule 8.4(d), which prohibits conduct prejudicial to the administration of justice.

I am now seeking the Court's intervention to review the Disciplinary Board's decision, as I believe that procedural due process was compromised and the evidence was not adequately considered, resulting in a miscarriage of justice.

*C. Procedural History of the Case*

I have been involved in a prolonged legal battle related to the protection of my rights and my family's rights following an academic and administrative dispute involving a state university and subsequent legal actions. In January 2024, I filed a discrimination complaint with the Pennsylvania Human Relations Commission (PHRC), citing procedural violations, retaliation, and discrimination by the university. The university, represented by their legal counsel, submitted responses to the PHRC that I assert were false and misleading, clearly violating Rule 8.4(c) (prohibiting dishonesty and misrepresentation) and Rule 8.4(d) (prohibiting conduct prejudicial to the administration of justice) under the Pennsylvania Rules of Professional Conduct.

On June 1, 2024, the Disciplinary Board of the Supreme Court of Pennsylvania issued a decision dismissing my complaint against the attorneys involved, justifying their decision by referencing the attorneys' duty to protect their client's interests. The Board's decision did not take into consideration the documented evidence I provided, such as email correspondence and official records that contradicted the attorneys' statements to the PHRC.

I contend that the Board's decision failed to maintain the principles of procedural fairness as outlined in Article V, Section 10(c) of the Pennsylvania Constitution, and disregarded unmistakable evidence of clear ethical violations. In response, I filed this timely appeal, requesting that the Supreme Court of Pennsylvania review the Board's decision and assess the implications for procedural due process and the professional accountability of legal practitioners.

This appeal follows the procedural timeline. It includes additional submissions that address the broader issues of fairness, transparency, and adherence to ethical standards under Pennsylvania law and judicial review.

## V. STANDARD OF REVIEW

I understand that this Court reviews the Disciplinary Board's decisions de novo in matters involving professional conduct and procedural due process, applying relevant constitutional and procedural laws. The standard set forth under Pennsylvania appellate practice allows for review if the decision was "arbitrary, capricious, an abuse of discretion, or otherwise not in accordance with law," similar to the principles found in general administrative review (5 U.S.C. § 706(2)(A)).

This Court reviews de novo whether procedural due process was observed in administrative proceedings. Any oversight or failure to exhaust procedural remedies by administrative bodies, such as those that affect a party's ability to present substantial evidence, can be challenged under the principles outlined in Pennsylvania law and relevant appellate practice.

## VI. SUMMARY OF ARGUMENT

**I.** The central issue in this case involves ensuring fairness, transparency, and adherence to established ethical and legal standards within the proceedings of the Disciplinary Board of the Supreme Court of Pennsylvania. The Board's dismissal of my complaint against the attorneys representing the state university overlooks documented evidence that refutes their claims, which undermined due process and professional accountability.

Under Rule 8.4(c) of the Pennsylvania Rules of Professional Conduct, attorneys are prohibited from engaging in dishonest conduct or misrepresentation. Despite this reality, the university's legal team made assertions that contradicted verifiable evidence, including an email I submitted demonstrating that a formal grade adjudication request was made on January 24, 2024. This directly challenges the attorneys' claim that no such request was made prior to the January 31, 2024's dismissal decision. The attorneys' assertion that I failed to complete two required courses was similarly false and unsupported by my academic record.

The Disciplinary Board's rationale—that the attorneys' statements were made in the interest of their client—sidesteps their duty to maintain honesty and fairness in proceedings, as mandated by Rule 8.4(d), which prohibits conduct prejudicial to the administration of justice. The Board's decision sets a troubling precedent by suggesting that attorneys may present falsehoods under the guise of advocacy without facing appropriate scrutiny or consequences.

This case raises important questions about the limits of advocacy, the role of state oversight bodies in upholding professional standards, and the necessity for procedural fairness. The failure to act on unambiguous evidence of misconduct erodes trust in the legal system and compromises the integrity of administrative and judicial processes. My appeal seeks to redress these failures and uphold the principles of due process, fairness, and accountability as enshrined in Pennsylvania law and professional conduct regulations.

II. A. Even if, contrary to the unmistakable evidence, the Board's decision to dismiss my complaint were to stand, the Board's determination that protecting client interests permits attorneys to make false statements cannot be reconciled with the relevant rules of professional conduct. Rule 8.4(c) specifically prohibits attorneys from engaging in dishonesty, fraud, deceit, or misrepresentation. Yet, the Board's decision overlooked evidence proving that the attorneys involved knowingly submitted false statements during proceedings.

The professional conduct rules plainly indicate when misrepresentation is prohibited, and Rule 8.4(d) explicitly bars conduct that is prejudicial to the administration of justice. The Board's decision, by excusing these acts, contradicts the objective of maintaining fairness and accountability within the legal profession.

The Board's rationale further conflicted with its own mandate by not addressing the requirement that the evidence be evaluated for truthfulness, a critical step in ensuring procedural justice. This oversight goes against the purpose of the rules, which are meant to uphold transparency and integrity in legal processes.

B. Should this Court find ambiguity in the Board's interpretation, such an interpretation is unreasonable and should be rejected. The Board's decision undermines the purpose of maintaining professional accountability and erodes public trust in the justice system. The dismissal failed to align with Rule 8.4(c) and 8.4(d) standards, suggesting a selective application that favors certain parties over others. This selective approach is arbitrary, capricious, and contrary to the ethical requirements outlined in professional conduct rules, as well as principles of fairness and due process.

**C.** Because the relevant rules of professional conduct do not permit blanket protection of client advocacy to include false statements, the conclusion reached based on objective evidence should be that the attorneys violated these standards. The evidence I submitted, including documented communications, plainly demonstrated that the attorneys' statements were false and that the Board's decision not to consider this evidence fails to uphold the ethical obligations of the legal profession. This Court should recognize that adherence to these rules is essential for ensuring a just and fair process.

**III.** The Disciplinary Board further erred in refusing to consider the procedural and due process violations evident in its handling of my complaint. The Board concluded that it could not address these issues substantively, implying that the presented evidence did not merit review. This reasoning overlooks that I, the Petitioner, undoubtedly raised these concerns, supported by documented submissions showing clear breaches of Rule 8.4(c) and Rule 8.4(d). The Board's decision acknowledged the existence of these claims but opted not to evaluate them fully, citing procedural limitations that unjustly restricted the consideration of key evidence.

The Board's dismissal does not negate the need for a thorough review of due process violations; such a refusal effectively denies fair examination and accountability. Moreover, the Supreme Court of Pennsylvania has recognized that procedural due process is essential in upholding fairness in administrative decisions.

A fundamental review by this Court is warranted as a matter of procedural justice. The Board's failure to consider substantive due process claims violates the principles of fairness enshrined in Article V, Section 10(c) of the Pennsylvania Constitution. The Board's limited review should not preclude the right to a full and impartial evaluation of evidence when rules of professional conduct and procedural fairness are at issue. Therefore, I respectfully request that this Court remand the case for a complete examination of due process and ethical breaches evident in the Board's initial decision.

# CHAPTER 14

# ARGUMENT

## I. THE STATUTORY FRAMEWORK CONFIRMS THAT STATE LAW CONTROLS WHETHER CONDUCT VIOLATES PROFESSIONAL STANDARDS OF HONESTY AND INTEGRITY

A. *The Pennsylvania Rules of Professional Conduct and applicable case law instruct that straightforward evidence and adherence to procedural fairness are paramount in disciplinary proceedings.*

The Pennsylvania Rules of Professional Conduct Rule 8.4(c) expressly prohibits attorneys from engaging in conduct involving dishonesty, fraud, deceit, or misrepresentation. It is a fundamental principle in both state and federal jurisprudence that rules of professional conduct are interpreted and applied in a manner consistent with maintaining public trust in the legal system (see *Office of Disciplinary Counsel v. Monsour*, 701 A.2d 556, Pa. 1997).

Courts have historically upheld that disciplinary bodies are bound to review unmistakable evidence of undeniable misconduct when determining whether an attorney's conduct meets the high standards set by the profession. The principle that state law, or in this case, professional standards of conduct, should guide such determinations aligns with rulings in cases such as *De Sylva v. Ballentine*, 351 U.S. 570 (1956), which underscored the importance of state law in determining questions within its purview.

The Supreme Court's ruling in *Gregory v. Ashcroft*, 501 U.S. 452, 461 (1991), emphasized that the Court should not lightly interfere in areas where state law traditionally governs, such as professional conduct regulations, without clear legislative direction. This reinforces that Pennsylvania's Rules should be interpreted with deference to their stated purpose of protecting the integrity of the legal system.

The Disciplinary Board's decision to dismiss my claims without fully engaging with the presented evidence contravenes these principles, constituting a failure to adhere to established rules of professional ethics and procedural due process, as required under Article V, Section 10(c) of the Pennsylvania Constitution.

*B. The Importance of Upholding State Law Over Federal Impositions in Professional Conduct Cases*

In the context of determining whether conduct violates professional ethics or rules, courts have consistently upheld that state law should take precedence unless there is a clear federal legislative intent to override it. This principle is supported by case law emphasizing that professional and ethical regulations are deeply rooted in state jurisdiction.

The Fourth Circuit's decision in *Ojo v. Lynch*, 813 F.3d 533 (2016), provides a closely related precedent illustrating this point. In *Ojo*, the court underscored that when determining whether a child qualifies as "adopted" for federal immigration purposes, state law, not federal definitions, or additional requirements, must govern. The court stated, "The term 'adopted' carries with it the understanding that adoption proceedings in this country are conducted by various state courts pursuant to state law," and emphasized that Congress did not delegate the interpretation of the term to federal agencies without explicitly stating so.

Applying this rationale to professional conduct in legal proceedings, it becomes evident that Pennsylvania state rules and standards should similarly control in determining whether attorneys' actions meet the ethical requirements set forth by Rule 8.4(c) and Rule 8.4(d) of the Pennsylvania Rules of Professional Conduct. The BIA's and other agencies' federal-level interpretations or decisions should not override these state-specific determinations unless a clear, unambiguous directive from Congress dictates otherwise, as established in *Gregory v. Ashcroft*, 501 U.S. 452 (1991). This case reaffirms that without a plain statement to the contrary, areas traditionally governed by state law—such as the regulation of professional ethics—remain under state jurisdiction.

Thus, the Disciplinary Board's reliance on federal interpretations that fail to consider or defer to state-specific rules undermine the established legal precedent that state law is the guiding framework in matters of professional conduct. As demonstrated in *Matter of Cross*, 26 I. & N. Dec. 485 (BIA 2015), interpretations must acknowledge that state law is dynamic and tailored to the local legal environment, underscoring that applying state law is not only legally appropriate but essential for fairness and consistency in upholding professional standards.

*C. Congress's Directives for Applying State Law in Federal Contexts are Established in Multiple Statutes*

Congress' approach of directing courts and federal agencies to apply state law when interpreting federal provisions is a long-standing practice. As recognized by the Supreme Court, while the scope of a federal right is a "federal question," the content may be determined by state law. *De Sylva v. Ballentine*, 351 U.S. 570, 580 (1956). This principle is vital for ensuring consistency and deference to state jurisdiction, particularly in areas traditionally under state control, such as family law and professional conduct.

For instance, under the Federal Tort Claims Act (FTCA), the federal government's liability is determined "in accordance with the law of the place where the act or omission occurred." 28 U.S.C. § 1346(b)(1). Courts have held that the FTCA "mandates application of state law to resolve questions of substantive liability." *Cannon v. United States*, 338 F.3d 1183, 1192 (10th Cir. 2003). This deference to state law allows for state-specific principles to inform federal liability, which reflected Congress's intent to maintain the state-federal balance.

A parallel approach is observed in constitutional tort cases brought under 42 U.S.C. § 1983. Through 42 U.S.C. § 1988, Congress explicitly directed courts to utilize state law to fill statutory gaps, such as the statute of limitations, when federal law is silent. *Baker v. Bd. of Regents of State of Kan.*, 991 F.2d 628, 630 (10th Cir. 1993). This practice ensures that state laws can enhance or limit procedural rights as recognized under federal statutes, maintaining harmony between state and federal systems.

The Sixth Circuit's decision in *Advance Stores Co. v. Refinishing Specialties, Inc.*, 188 F.3d 408 (6th Cir. 1999), provides further support. The Lanham Act, which governs trademark rights, states that a registered trademark's "incontestability" is subject to "rights acquired under the law of any State or Territory." 15 U.S.C. § 1065. The Sixth Circuit adhered to this directive, rejecting the imposition of a federal common law definition, and instead applying Kentucky law to determine rights acquisition. *Advance Stores*, 188 F.3d at 412-13.

These precedents reinforce that the Immigration and Nationality Act (INA), which specifies that the "law of the child's [or father's] residence or domicile" determines legitimation, must be interpreted in accordance with state law. See *Ojo v. Lynch*, 813 F.3d 533, 540 (4th Cir. 2016). The district court's and BIA's imposition of a biological requirement absent from state law disregards this principle, effectively creating a federal standard not intended by Congress. The statutory language of § 1101(b)(1)(C) plainly requires adherence to state law, just as other statutes have directed deference to state interpretations. This analysis underscores that Kansas law, which considers adoption as legitimation, should control the determination of whether a child is "legitimated" for federal purposes.

*D. Deference to established legal and procedural rules upholds the integrity of judicial oversight and professional conduct*

It is well-established that statutory and professional codes should be interpreted and applied in a manner consistent with their fundamental objectives, which include promoting justice and maintaining public trust in the legal system. In my case, Pennsylvania law and professional conduct rules exist to ensure that attorneys act with integrity and in a manner that supports, rather than undermines, the administration of justice. See *Office of Disciplinary Counsel v. Anonymous Attorney A*, 714 A.2d 402 (Pa. 1998) (emphasizing the importance of truthfulness and ethical behavior in legal practice). The Disciplinary Board's decision, which failed to address unmistakable evidence of misrepresentation and procedural violations, runs counter to these objectives.

The core purpose of rule pertaining to attorney conduct, such as Rule 8.4(c) and Rule 8.4(d), is to ensure that attorneys do not engage in dishonest or prejudicial conduct that affects the administration of justice. These provisions align with the broader judicial principle that "truth-seeking is the cornerstone of the legal process," as articulated in cases like *Commonwealth v. Johnson*, 966 A.2d 523 (Pa. 2009). Upholding these rules fosters public confidence in the legal system. This ensures that parties to legal proceedings are treated equitably.

The application of these rules must reflect the reality that professional misconduct can undermine due process and obstruct a fair resolution. When state entities disregard evidence and fail to act impartially, they compromise the judicial system's role as a neutral arbiter. My case demonstrates that adherence to these rules would affirm that all parties, regardless of status, have their claims evaluated based on the merits and truth of their arguments, thus reinforcing public trust in legal institutions.

By failing to consider documented evidence and by accepting misleading representations, the Board's approach contravenes the very principles these ethical rules aim to safeguard. This oversight also undermines the protective mechanisms meant to address misconduct and ensure accountability within the legal profession. See *In re Conduct of Capps*, 968 P.2d 47 (Or. 1998) (emphasizing the critical role of impartiality and diligence in disciplinary proceedings).

Interpreting the relevant rules and statutes to support rigorous adherence to ethical and procedural standards not only aligns with established legal norms but also serves the broader purpose of maintaining justice and protecting individuals from unfair treatment within the legal system.

*E. Pennsylvania law affirms evidence of misconduct in this case*

Applying Pennsylvania's Rules of Professional Conduct and procedural laws compels the conclusion that the actions of the attorneys involved in my case were contrary to ethical and legal standards. The Pennsylvania Rules of Professional Conduct, specifically Rule 8.4(c), prohibit any conduct involving dishonesty, fraud, deceit, or misrepresentation. Rule 8.4(d) further prohibits conduct that is prejudicial to the administration of justice. In my case, documented evidence, including email correspondence and official records, demonstrate that the attorneys involved made false statements during formal proceedings before the Pennsylvania Human Relations Commission (PHRC), which violated these professional obligations.

Under Pennsylvania law, misrepresentation, particularly when it impacts judicial or quasi-judicial proceedings, is taken seriously, and viewed as an affront to the principles of justice and fairness. The courts in Pennsylvania have long held that upholding ethical standards is essential for maintaining public trust in the legal profession. See *Office of Disciplinary Counsel v. Anonymous Attorney A*, 714 A.2d 402 (Pa. 1998), where the Pennsylvania Supreme Court underscored the importance of attorneys maintaining honesty and integrity. This aligns with the principle that state legal mechanisms are in place to protect parties from clear abuse within legal processes and to ensure that justice is administered fairly.

The evidence I submitted, showing discrepancies between the university's formal responses and documented facts, illustrates a violation of these ethical principles. My case, therefore, presents a clear instance where adherence to state law and ethical rules should result in accountability for those who have breached these professional standards. This approach would affirm the commitment of Pennsylvania's legal system to uphold justice and prevent misconduct.

Adherence to Pennsylvania law, particularly the ethical standards set by the Rules of Professional Conduct, supports the position that the attorneys' actions were inconsistent with their professional obligations. The documented evidence

should lead to a finding that these actions violated the principles of honesty and fairness, as mandated by the relevant rules
and statutes.

*F. The Petitioner is not constrained by a single standard in
addressing the procedural and ethical violations in this case*

In prior proceedings, the opposing parties argued that
focusing solely on the attorneys' misrepresentations would
obscure broader issues and evidently overlap with other applicable standards under the Rules of Professional Conduct.
Although the Disciplinary Board did not specifically rely on this
argument in their decision, it is crucial to address this point as
it is both misleading and inconsequential.

First, the argument is misleading because state ethics laws,
including the Pennsylvania Rules of Professional Conduct,
outline distinct yet complementary obligations that legal
professionals must observe. For instance, while Rule 8.4(c)
addresses dishonesty, fraud, deceit, or misrepresentation, Rule
8.4(d) ensures conduct must not be a prejudice to the administration of justice. These rules, although addressing distinct
aspects of attorney conduct, are not mutually exclusive.
Violating one does not preclude the violation of another;
instead, they often operate together to uphold the integrity of
the legal process.

overlapping standards and clear violations do not dilute the
gravity of each infraction. For example, while Rule 8.4(c)
focuses on truthful representation, Rule 3.3 emphasizes candor
toward tribunals, and Rule 1.3 stresses the duty of diligence.
Thus, addressing misrepresentation under Rule 8.4(c) does not
negate an argument that Rule 8.4(d) was also violated by
conduct that undermined procedural fairness and due process.

The central concern here is that the Disciplinary Board's
decision did not acknowledge or engage with these intercon-
nected breaches despite substantial evidence. The documented

inaccuracies presented by the attorneys in response to the PHRC should have invoked scrutiny under multiple provisions of the ethical code. This failure by the Board to thoroughly investigate or apply relevant rules effectively results in a procedural deficiency that warrants this appeal.

What matters in this context is that the documented evidence demonstrates ethical violations that align with multiple sections of the Rules of Professional Conduct. My claims, under Rule 8.4(c) and 8.4(d), are substantiated. They show that the attorneys' actions were not only dishonest but prejudicial to the administration of justice. The Supreme Court of Pennsylvania should therefore remand the matter for a thorough examination that carefully considers the full scope of applicable ethical standards.

## II. NO RULE OR STANDARD IMPOSES A BLANKET REQUIREMENT EXCLUDING ALTERNATIVE EVIDENCE TO ESTABLISH MISCONDUCT

Even if it were assumed that the Disciplinary Board's decision to require a strict interpretation of advocacy principles was reasonable, the imposition of a rigid standard that disregards straightforward evidence of dishonesty conflicts with the intent and language of the ethical rules. Specifically, Rule 8.4(c) of the Pennsylvania Rules of Professional Conduct outlines that an attorney's conduct involving dishonesty, fraud, deceit, or misrepresentation is prohibited. There is no clause or precedent that suggests only certain types of evidence, such as direct admissions, must be considered to prove such a violation.

The Board's approach in dismissing the complaint without a thorough investigation into the documented inconsistencies undermines the principles of fairness and integrity that these professional rules aim to safeguard. If there were any perceived ambiguity in how these rules should be applied, the conclusion that no action should be taken when unmistakable evidence exists would be unreasonable and counter to the purpose of these standards.

The decision to dismiss the complaint solely based on a narrow interpretation, which ignores documented evidence contrary to the attorneys' statements, does not align with the mandate to ensure justice is served without prejudice or bias. This appeal seeks to clarify that no blanket requirement or restriction exists that would exclude credible, documented evidence from being considered in matters alleging violations of professional conduct rules.

*A. The Language and Context of Relevant Rules Do Not Impose Additional Burdens Beyond Documented Evidence*

The Disciplinary Board's decision to dismiss my complaint against the attorneys' actions relied on an unwarranted interpretation that overlooks the plain language and context of the Pennsylvania Rules of Professional Conduct, particularly Rule 8.4(c) and Rule 8.4(d). The Board's approach effectively imposed an unreasonable burden of proof that extends beyond what is required under these rules.

Rule 8.4(c) explicitly prohibits attorneys from engaging in any form of dishonesty, deceit, or misrepresentation, while Rule 8.4(d) prohibits conduct prejudicial to the administration of justice. The plain language of these rules does not contain a provision or implication that excludes documented evidence from being sufficient to establish a violation. By dismissing my complaint, despite substantial documented evidence, which demonstrates misrepresentation by the attorneys, the Board applied an overly restrictive standard inconsistent with both the text and purpose of these professional rules.

The Board's analysis also stands contrary to established principles that discourage unnecessary additions or interpretations that alter the meaning of a statute or rule. See *Ela v. Destefano*, 869 F.3d 1198, 1202 (11th Cir. 2017) ("Where Congress knows how to say something but chooses not to, its silence is controlling"). Similarly, the analysis applied in cases such as *Fish v. Kobach*, 840 F.3d 710, 740 (10th Cir. 2016), underscores that silence or omission should not be read as an implicit requirement when the statutory or rule language is clear.

While the Board referenced precedent and regulations, none justifies ignoring documented evidence that supports claims of misrepresentation. The decision not only contradicts the spirit of the relevant rules but also undermines the procedural fairness and integrity expected in disciplinary proceedings.

*B. Imposing an Unreasonable Standard Without Basis Undermines Fairness and Due Process*

Even if there were any ambiguity in interpreting Rule 8.4(c) or Rule 8.4(d), it would be unreasonable to impose a blanket standard that effectively dismisses documented evidence of misconduct or misrepresentation without consideration. The Board's approach in dismissing my complaint against the attorneys involved fails to account for fundamental principles of fairness and procedural due process. Any interpretation that denies documented and credible evidence undermines the essential purpose of maintaining justice and professional integrity.

Courts have emphasized that interpretations or applications of rules that fail to align with their underlying purpose can be considered arbitrary or capricious. See, e.g., *Harbert v. Healthcare Servs. Grp., Inc.*, 391 F.3d 1140, 1149 (10th Cir. 2004) ("Courts must guard against interpretations that might defeat a statute's purpose."). Similarly, applying a standard that discounts well-documented evidence or fails to consider evidence on an individual basis is contrary to both legal precedent and ethical practice.

In previous cases addressing similar issues, courts have noted that overbroad or rigid applications of rules, particularly when based on general fears or administrative convenience, do not justify dismissing claims that are otherwise meritorious. For example, in *Gonzalez-Martinez v. Department of Homeland Security*, 677 F. Supp. 2d 1233 (D. Utah 2009), the court highlighted that rigid, one-size-fits-all approaches place undue emphasis on generalized concerns (such as fraud) and lead to the unwarranted dismissal of legitimate claims. The court ruled that such practices improperly overlooked Congress's or the rule's aim, which, in that case, was family unity; similarly, in professional conduct, it is ensuring honesty and upholding justice.

The Board's decision in my case, dismissing the documented and substantiated evidence of misrepresentation, reflects an overreach that places an undue burden on petitioners like me while effectively shielding improper conduct. Such a standard, if left unchecked, would erode trust in the system and the very purpose of professional conduct rules—to maintain fairness, transparency, and justice.

*C. The Board's Dismissal of My Complaint Was Erroneous and Contrary to Established Professional Standards*

The analysis and the evidence presented show that the Board's dismissal of my complaint, which involved demonstrable misrepresentations made by the attorneys representing the university, was unjustified and erroneous. Under a correct application of Rule 8.4(c) of the Pennsylvania Rules of Professional Conduct, attorneys are prohibited from engaging in dishonesty, fraud, deceit, or misrepresentation. The evidence I provided demonstrated clear instances where the attorneys misrepresented the facts related to my academic dismissal and the timeline of the grade adjudication request.

The Board's decision to overlook this evidence, dismissing my complaint without sufficient justification, runs counter to the purpose of maintaining integrity and trust within the legal profession. A proper reading of Rule 8.4(d), which prohibits conduct that can be prejudicial to the administration of justice, should have resulted in the Board acknowledging the implications of such misrepresentations. Instead, the dismissal reflects a failure to uphold these critical professional standards, effectively shielding behavior that compromises fairness and the justice system's credibility.

Given the clear documentation I submitted, including verified communications and records refuting the attorneys' claims, the Board's failure to consider this evidence in its decision constitutes an error in judgment. This not only undermines public trust in the oversight of legal professionals but also disregards the fundamental aim of the rules—to promote honesty and prevent conduct that damages the legal system's integrity.

## III. THE DISCIPLINARY BOARD WRONGLY REFUSED TO ADDRESS MY PROCEDURAL DUE PROCESS CLAIM

If the Supreme Court of Pennsylvania agrees that the Pennsylvania Rules of Professional Conduct were violated, leading to misconduct by the attorneys involved in my case, it need go no further. However, if the Court accepts the Board's conclusions as valid, this case should still be remanded for further consideration because the Board improperly refused to address my constitutional claims concerning due process violations.

I argued before the Disciplinary Board that the failure to investigate the attorneys' misrepresentations violated my right to procedural due process and compromised the fairness of the administrative process. This is a significant constitutional claim, which implies fundamental justice and requires rigorous review. The Supreme Court has emphasized that due process must be safeguarded, especially when administrative decisions affect rights and reputations. See, e.g., *Mathews v. Eldridge*, 424 U.S. 319, 332 (1976).

The Board's refusal to address my due process claim was improper for two reasons. First, as demonstrated by the records I submitted, the procedural arguments were raised in my filings and during correspondence with the Board. Second, as a matter of Pennsylvania law, exhaustion of administrative remedies does not apply when an individual seeks judicial review to protect constitutional rights—particularly when procedural due process violations are alleged. See *Pennsylvania Coal Co. v. Mahon*, 260 U.S. 393 (1922).

Thus, even if the Court were to uphold the Board's dismissal of the complaints based on other grounds, it should be remanded for proper consideration of the constitutional issues, which go to the heart of maintaining a fair and just system.

*A. I Raised My Constitutional Claims Before the Disciplinary Board*

After the Disciplinary Board dismissed my complaint on June 1, 2024, I reached out to board executives and intake Counsel members via mail and raised several issues, including the clear violation of my due process rights. I not only presented my constitutional claims to the Board, as evidenced by their own decision, I also offered new evidence to support my claim against attorney misconduct. I filed a new complaint with additional materials. However, the Board neither responded nor acknowledged my new complaint. In their decision, the Board claims that rules of professional conduct are limited in scope.

The Pennsylvania Rules of Professional Conduct (RPC) establish ethical standards for attorneys in the state. While the Disciplinary Board may assert that these rules are limited in scope, several cases demonstrate their broad applicability. In *Office of Disciplinary Counsel v. Cynthia A. Baldwin,* 225 A.3d 817 (Pa. 2020), the Pennsylvania Supreme Court found that attorney Cynthia Baldwin violated multiple RPC provisions, including Rules 1.1 (Competence), 1.6(a) (Confidentiality of Information), 1.7(a) (Conflict of Interest: Current Clients), and 8.4(d) (Misconduct). Baldwin's representation of Penn State University and its officials during grand jury proceedings related to child abuse allegations was deemed incompetent and conflicted, leading to a public reprimand.

In *Office of Disciplinary Counsel v. Jonathan F. Altman,* 228 A.3d 508 (Pa. 2020), Attorney Jonathan Altman was disbarred for engaging in prohibited sexual relations with a client, failing to protect the client's interests in mutual business dealings, and abusing the legal system to pursue unjustified expenses and fees. His actions violated several RPC provisions, which underscored the rules' comprehensive reach in governing attorney conduct. *Office of Disciplinary Counsel v. Anonymous Attorney A,* 714 A.2d 402 (Pa. 1998) addressed the element of scienter necessary to establish a prima facie violation of RPC 8.4(c) concerning misrepresentation. The court held that a violation is shown where misrepresentation was knowingly made or made with reckless ignorance of its truth or falsity, which highlighted the RPC's role in maintaining honesty and integrity within the profession.

The Board acknowledged my complaint while concluding that it lacked jurisdiction to address the issues raised, stating that "some actions which one might consider 'improper' or 'unethical' do not violate any of the pertinent rules." This acknowledgment is inconsistent with the Board's conclusion that the attorneys did not violate any professional conduct rules, implicating that I had not properly presented these claims. It must be noted that the Board's response did not dismiss the existence of my constitutional concerns. However, it deferred action to the PHRC or other tribunals, due to its perceived limitations in the matter. However, the Board's conclusion is inconsistent with established laws.

In re Anonymous No. 5 D.B. 93 (Pa. 1993), an attorney was disciplined for conduct that may not have been explicitly defined as unethical within the RPC but was still deemed to undermine public confidence in the legal profession. The disciplinary Board emphasized that even actions that do not squarely fall under a specific rule can still constitute misconduct if they tarnish the integrity of the profession. In *Office of Disciplinary Counsel v. Price,* 732 A.2d 599 (Pa. 1999), the Pennsylvania Supreme Court found that while an attorney's conduct might not fit squarely within the language of the Rules of Professional Conduct, it still violated broader professional standards. The court noted that behavior that undermines public trust or reflects poorly on the legal profession can be sanctionable, which illustrates that ethical violations can extend beyond narrowly defined acts.

In *Office of Disciplinary Counsel v. Anonymous Attorney,* 715 A.2d 402 (Pa. 1998), the court further discussed the application of Rule 8.4, which addresses conduct involving dishonesty, fraud, deceit, or misrepresentation. The case demonstrates that even if an attorney's behavior does not clearly violate a specific rule, it can still be deemed unethical if it involves conduct contrary to justice, honesty, or good morals. Moreover, *In re Johnson,* 60 A.3d 205 (Pa. 2013), a case that outlined how conduct not explicitly stated in the RPC can still lead to disciplinary action if it is considered detrimental to the reputation of the legal profession, the court emphasized that maintaining public confidence is a key objective. Attorneys are held to a standard of behavior that may encompass actions beyond those detailed in specific rules.

The previous cases illustrate that while some conduct might not be directly spelled out as a violation of specific rules, it can still be deemed unethical or improper when considering the broader objectives and spirit of professional responsibility. These cases challenge the notion that actions perceived as "improper" are always outside the purview of disciplinary measures, if not explicitly covered by the rules. These cases illustrate that the Pennsylvania Rules of Professional Conduct are applied broadly to various aspects of legal practice, including competence, confidentiality, conflicts of interest, and overall professional integrity.

The Board's blanket dismissal of my original complaint and its failure to acknowledge my concerns and the new complaint filed to their office failed to address the depth of my constitutional argument, which challenged the procedural handling and due process violations that I encountered. Certainly, courts have discretionary power to consider arguments raised by individuals or amici, particularly when they pertain to jurisdictional matters, issues of fundamental rights, or other extraordinary circumstances. See *In re McGough*, 737 F.3d 1268, 1277 n.8 (10th Cir. 2013). This case presents such exceptional circumstances, as my argument was directly tied to procedural and substantive due process, aiming to ensure fairness in how claims of professional misconduct were addressed by the Pennsylvania Disciplinary Board.

The Board wrongly concluded that I did not sufficiently raise any issues, which can "substantiate a violation of the Rules of Professional Conduct based on [my] allegations." The Board's refusal to acknowledge my constitutional argument is prejudicial to my case before the PHRC, as it undermines the violations that led to my unlawful dismissal from the nursing program. In my initial and follow-up filings, I explicitly referenced procedural due process violations, citing how the Board's failure to consider my presented evidence compromised fundamental fairness. According to *Forest Guardians v. U.S. Forest Serv.*, 641 F.3d 423, 430 (10th Cir. 2011), a party's argument needs only be raised in a way that allows the agency to meaningfully consider it. My filings met this standard by articulating the legal basis of my due process challenge and citing relevant constitutional provisions, ensuring that the Board was put on notice.

Finally, a more detailed presentation of these constitutional issues to the Board would not have changed the outcome, as the Board itself indicated that it lacked the authority to resolve constitutional matters or matters of law or fact. Where further action would be futile, exhaustion is not required. See, e.g., *Baquera v. Longshore*, 948 F. Supp. 2d 1258, 1259 (D. Colo. 2013). This demonstrates that I exhausted my arguments sufficiently for judicial review. The matter now warrants this Court's attention to prevent ongoing violations of my due process rights.

*B. Disciplining an Attorney for Conduct that Violates a Specific Rule*

The Board claims that "an attorney can only be disciplined for conduct that clearly violates a specific Rule." However, case law demonstrates that disciplinary bodies and courts often interpret the Rules of Professional Conduct considering broader ethical standards. Attorneys can face discipline for conduct that may not fit neatly within a specific rule but violates the spirit or overarching purpose of the rules. For instance, in *Office of Disciplinary Counsel v. Duffield*, 644 A.2d 1186 (Pa. 1994), the Pennsylvania Supreme Court held that an attorney's behavior could be disciplined even if it did not clearly violate a specific rule but nonetheless constituted misconduct that undermined the public's confidence in the legal system. The court emphasized that professional conduct standards are meant to uphold the integrity of the profession. Thus, violations can be based on conduct that compromises this integrity, even if not explicitly outlined in a particular rule.

*In re Anonymous No. 14 D.B. 93* (Pa. 1993), the court noted that discipline for conduct that did not explicitly fall under a specific Rule of Professional Conduct can still be deemed detrimental to the integrity of the legal profession. The case reinforced the principle that disciplinary actions are not limited to clear-cut rule violations but can extend to actions that reflect poorly on the legal profession. In *Office of Disciplinary Counsel v. John T. Rogers*, 537 A.2d 1076 (Pa. 1988), the court disciplined an attorney for conduct that was found to be unethical, even though it was not specifically prohibited by any single rule. This case demonstrated that the overall purpose of the rules is to promote justice and integrity. They can also serve as the basis for disciplinary action.

*In re Robert L. Surrick*, 749 A.2d 441 (Pa. 2000), the court highlighted that conduct that brings disrepute to the legal profession can result in discipline even if it does not align perfectly with a specified rule. The court noted that attorneys are expected to uphold a standard of behavior that ensures public confidence, and deviation from this standard can be grounds for discipline. These cases show that while clear rule violations are often easier to identify and enforce, attorneys can be disciplined for conduct that contravenes the overarching principles and integrity of the legal profession, even if it is not specifically mentioned in a particular rule. This reflects the idea that the ethical standards of the profession encompass more than just the explicit language of the rules.

*C. The Role of Evidence in Disciplinary Complaint Against an Attorney*

In its dismissal decision, the Board notes: "This office must assess matters complained of as to whether any potential disciplinary violation involved is established by a preponderance of the evidence." However, the standard of proof for disciplinary actions against attorneys often requires that violations be established by a preponderance of the evidence. This approach hints that it is more likely than not that the alleged conduct occurred and constituted a violation. Here, the Board undermined the relevance of the evidence I presented while acknowledging the need for preponderance of evidence to substantiate my allegations.

In *Office of Disciplinary Counsel v. Kiesewetter*, 889 A.2d 47 (Pa. 2005), the Pennsylvania Supreme Court affirmed that disciplinary proceedings use the "preponderance of the evidence" standard, which is a lower burden than "beyond a reasonable doubt" (used in criminal cases). The Office of Disciplinary Counsel had to show that it was more likely than not that the attorney's conduct violated the applicable rules. This case underscores that the focus in disciplinary matters is on whether the evidence shows that the allegations are more probable than not.

In *Office of Disciplinary Counsel v. Lucarini*, 472 A.2d 186 (Pa. 1983), the court held that attorney disciplinary proceedings are civil in nature. Therefore, the preponderance of the evidence standard applies. This standard requires that the evidence presented must lead to the conclusion that the facts at issue are more likely true than not.

Likewise, in the case *Office of Disciplinary Counsel v. Campbell*, 345 A.2d 616 (Pa. 1975), the court outlined that disciplinary boards must assess whether the facts alleged can be substantiated by a preponderance of the evidence before taking any action. The court indicated that it is necessary for the evidence to meet this threshold to support findings of violations of professional conduct rules. *In re Disciplinary Proceedings Against Raymond S. Alberts*, 453 A.2d 1189 (Pa. 1982), the court emphasized that the burden of proof lies with the disciplinary counsel to demonstrate violations of the Rules of Professional Conduct by a preponderance of the evidence. The evidence must be credible and sufficient to convince the tribunal that the violation occurred more likely than not.

These cases demonstrate that the preponderance of the evidence standard is an essential aspect of disciplinary proceedings against attorneys. This standard ensures that there is enough weight in the evidence presented to justify disciplinary action while acknowledging that the process does not require proof beyond a reasonable doubt. The board's refusal to acknowledge the evidence presented constitutes a miscarried of justice, as it undermines the very core of my argument, which is the email evidence I presented.

*D. Exhaustion Is Not Required When an Intra-Agency Appeal Is Optional*

The Board claims that the issues I raised are more appropriate for the PHRC tribunal to consider and determine. This argument presupposes that I must exhaust all remedies before the Board can address the issues I raised in my complaint. However, exhaustion of remedies was not legally required in my case.

The court's conclusion on exhaustion runs counter to the Supreme Court's clear guidance that parties challenging agency actions under the Administrative Procedure Act (APA) are not obligated to pursue optional intra-agency appeals. See *Darby v. Cisneros*, 509 U.S. 137, 147 (1993). According to *Darby*, once mandatory intra-agency appeals have been exhausted, a federal court must entertain the challenge. Requiring additional exhaustion contradicts the explicit language of the APA. Id.

Applying this principle indicates that the Board was obligated to consider my constitutional claims. When facing a denial or adverse decision by a state agency, any subsequent appeal within that agency is discretionary. Therefore, I was not mandated to exhaust any additional procedural steps before seeking judicial review, as the appeals process was optional.

The procedural timeline of my case supports this position. When I submitted my complaints to the disciplinary board, they issued their final decision without adequately addressing my constitutional and due process concerns. The issues I raised were not considered in depth, despite being articulated through detailed submissions and relevant evidence. My constitutional claims emerged more clearly upon the final decision when it became evident that procedural due process had been compromised.

The logic applied by the D.C. Circuit in *CSX Transportation, Inc. v. Surface Transportation Board*, 584 F.3d 1076 (D.C. Cir. 2009), is instructive. In *CSX*, the petitioner's challenge arose only after the issuance of a final rule, which makes it impractical to argue that exhaustion was necessary for issues that surfaced post-decision. The D.C. Circuit found that requiring the petitioner to pursue an optional petition for rehearing would contravene the *Darby* precedent. The same rationale applies here: my constitutional challenges materialized upon the issuance of the final decision, which makes prior exhaustion irrelevant.

The Board's focus on whether I exhausted available remedies in front of other tribunals, notably the PHRC, imposed an undue burden, which effectively rendered an optional process mandatory, a requirement that *Darby* explicitly forbids. This misapplication transformed an otherwise discretionary appeal process to the present Court into an obligatory one, infringing upon the principles established by *Darby*.

The district court's reliance on *Garcia-Carbajal v. Holder*, 625

F.3d 1233 (10th Cir. 2010), does not alter this conclusion. *Garcia-Carbajal* pertained to a removal order where BIA appeal was mandatory under 8 U.S.C. § 1252(d)(1). My case involves no such compulsory process. Therefore, my claims were properly brought before the Board. As such, exhaustion, lack of authority, or lack of jurisdiction to determine law for fact should not have precluded their consideration of my complaint due to the nature of the evidence I presented.

# AFTERWORD

The dismissal judgment rendered by the disciplinary board should be overturned. This Court should remand the matter with instructions to ensure a comprehensive review of the procedural and substantive violations raised. Specifically, the board's handling of the case demonstrates failures in applying due process principles and evaluating evidence thoroughly, which has prejudiced my position and infringed upon my rights under Pennsylvania law and constitutional mandates.

Alternatively, if this Court does not find sufficient grounds to directly reverse the board's decision, it should vacate the prior judgment and remand the matter to allow for a detailed examination of the constitutional claims. This reconsideration would address the failure to acknowledge key evidence and the misapplication of professional conduct standards that resulted in significant procedural lapses and breaches of fairness.

Remanding for a fresh and unbiased analysis is crucial to safeguard my right to due process and reinforce the integrity of the disciplinary review system. The Court's intervention is necessary to correct these deficiencies, ensure transparency, and uphold the rule of law in a manner that restores confidence in the judicial process.

Date: November 8, 2024, Respectfully submitted,

/s/Oliver-Johnson

CERTIFICATION OF COMLIANCE WITH WORD COUNT LIMITS

PURSUANT TO Pa. R.A.P. 910(c)

The Undersigned, Oliver-Johnson, certifies that the body of the foregoing Brief filed in this matter contains a total of 8,702 words as recorded by the Word processing program.

Dated: November 8, 2024, Respectfully submitted,

/s/Oliver-Johnson

—————————————————

Oliver-Johnson

# CERTIFICATE OF COMPLIANCE

I HEREBY CERTIFY that this brief complies with the word count limitation set forth in Pa.R.A.P. 2135(a). This brief contains 8,702 words, excluding the supplementary sections that do not count towards the word limit, as determined by the word count function of the word processing software used to prepare this document.

/s/Oliver-Johnson
Oliver-Johnson

*Submitted by: Oliver-Johnson*

Signature: __/s/Oliver-Johnson_____

Name: Oliver-Johnson

# CERTIFICATE OF SERVICE

I HEREBY CERTIFY that on November 8, 2024, I filed the foregoing document with the Clerk of the Supreme Court of Pennsylvania through the Court's electronic filing system, PACfile (via The Unified Judicial System of Pennsylvania Web Portal).

Participants in this case who are registered users of the electronic filing system will be served through that system. Any participants who are not registered users will be served via e-mail/regular mail.

Date: November 8, 2024

/s/Oliver-Johnson

_____

Appellant

123 My Address

My Town, Pennsylvania 0000

# PART FIVE
# EVIDENCE OF PA
# DISCIPLINARY
# BOARD
# MISCONDUCT

## OFFICIAL LETTERS, EMAILS, AND OTHER IMAGES

This case is well documented. The issues raised in the present context are based on established facts. See the author statement in the next page to learn more about the nature of the documents featured in this publication.

# AUTHOR STATEMENT

THE FOLLOWING pages contains information and contents that reflect true events. Considering that the Disciplinary Board of the Supreme Court of Pennsylvania is a publicly funded entity [institution], we [the author, the editor, and the publisher] have not redacted or altered the names and job titles of individuals mentioned in official letters, institutional policies, and any communications we received from the noted entities. The documents included in this publication were legally obtained either as a direct recipient of these communications or as a concerned citizen seeking accountability from a public institution. Furthermore, it is our [Oliver-Johnson family] good faith understanding that the officials referenced in this matter, including those affiliated with state agencies, qualify as public figures in their professional capacity, given their roles in the judicial system, public education, government oversight, and public administration.

# ATTORNEYS MADE FALSE STATEMENTS

**DUE PROCESS VIOLATIONS**

**FALSE STATEMENT TO A TRIBUNAL**

11. Denied as stated. On February 7, 2024, Respondent informed Complainant that it would conduct a grade adjudication, despite the fact that Complainant had not requested a grade adjudication prior to her January 31, 2024, academic dismissal letter from the College of Nursing. By way of further response, Respondent informed Complainant that, pursuant to Penn State policy, she could request a Leave of Absence in order to maintain access to her Penn State email account and other amenities because Complainant had not registered for any classes for the Spring 2024 semester at that time.

Respectfully submitted,

**BUCHANAN INGERSOLL & ROONEY PC**

*/s/ George C. Morrison*
George C. Morrison, Esq. (PA 203223)
Keith M. Lee, Esq. (PA 330237)
Andrew T. Simmons, Esq. (PA 331973)
Two Liberty Place
50 S. 16th Street, Suite 3200
Philadelphia, PA 19102
(215) 665-3909

**PROFESSIONAL MISCONDUCT BY THE ATTORNEYS**

Dated: July 15, 2024                    *Counsel for Respondent*

# EVIDENCE THAT ATTORNEYS MADE FALSE STATEMENTS

DUE PROCESS VIOLATIONS EVIDENCE

**From:** Oliver, Germine A <goblen5027@psu.edu>
**Sent:** Wednesday, January 24, 2024 3:28 PM
**To:** Hupcey, Judith E <jhupcey@psu.edu>; Badzek, Laurie <lzb340@psu.edu>; Matter, Sheri <sxm1898@psu.edu>; Wright Watson, Denita Renee <Denita@psu.edu>; Adair, Suzanne <sca917@psu.edu>; Fong, Duncan King-Hoi <i2v@psu.edu>; Grad Dean's Office <graddeansoffice@psu.edu>; Oman, Tabitha <txo5152@psu.edu>
**Subject:** Grade Adjudication request

Hello,

To whom it may concern.

Below is my formal request for a grade adjudication in the N596 independent study (Fall 2023).

The grade received violates school policy 47-20. The instructor did not provide a written (paper or electronic form) notification of the basis for grades to me on or before the first class meeting.

Also, I have been informed in an email correspondence by a representative from the office of Affirmative Action that I am being terminated from the nursing program for missing previously specified deadlines. This is another excuse to justify a blatant discriminatory act against my person at Penn State University. I intend to challenge these unsubstantiated claims as vigorously as Penn State policy guidelines would allow. It is my understanding that there are no such stipulations neither in school policy nor in the student handbook for the DNP program. I completed all the benchmarks and other requirements, as specified in the DNP program and within the prescribed timeline, except for the oral presentation, which is beyond my purview.

I intend to appeal any arbitrary decisions if and when they are communicated to me officially.


Please see attached document for the grade adjudication.


Germine Oliver

1/24/2024, 4:

# PENNSYLVANIA DISCIPLINARY BOARD SOUGHT TO SHIELD ATTORNEYS

Thomas J. Farrell
Chief Disciplinary Counsel

Raymond S. Wierciszewski
Deputy Chief Disciplinary Counsel

Jana M. Palko
Counsel-in-Charge, Central Intake
Frick Building, Ste. 1300
437 Grant Street
Pittsburgh, PA 15219
(412) 565-3173

THE DISCIPLINARY BOARD
OF THE
SUPREME COURT OF PENNSYLVANIA

OFFICE OF DISCIPLINARY COUNSEL
www.padisciplinaryboard.org

Intake Counsel

Robin B. Godfrey
Elizabeth J. Rubin
1601 Market St., Ste. 3320
Philadelphia, PA 19103-2337
(215) 560-6296

Dana M. Pirone
820 Adams Ave., Ste. 170
Trooper, PA 19403
(610) 650-8210

Anna M. Ciardi
Rebecca K. Leventopoulos
Samuel F. Napoli
Frick Building, Ste. 1300
437 Grant Street
Pittsburgh, PA 15219
(412) 565-3173

October 9, 2024

*PERSONAL AND CONFIDENTIAL*
Germine Oliver

Re: Complaints against
George Charles Morrison, Esquire (File # C1-24-723)
Andrew Thomas Simmons, Esquire (File # C1-24-724)
Keith Michael Lee, Esquire (File # C1-24-725)

Dear Ms. Oliver:

After reviewing the complaints against George Charles Morrison, Esquire, Andrew Thomas Simmons, Esquire, and Keith Michael Lee, Esquire, our office has determined that the complaints warrant dismissal for the reasons stated below.

In the complaints, you state, among other things, that Mr. Morrison, Mr. Simmons, and Mr. Lee are the opposing attorneys in your Pennsylvania Human Relations Commission (PHRC) matter against Penn State Ross and Carol Nese College of Nursing under Case No. 202317185. Your complaint to the PHRC concerns whether you did or did not submit a formal request for a grade adjudication prior to the issuance of the January 31, 2024 academic dismissal letter. You state that you emailed the formal request on January 24, 2024; however, the attorneys take a different position in their client's July 15, 2024 formal response. Thus, you believe that the record in the PHRC proceeding does not accurately represent the factual circumstances as to your January 24, 2024 submission. You ask that this office to, among other things, direct the attorneys to retract the false statements and information they provided to the PHRC.

The Rules of Professional Conduct are limited in scope, and express specific prohibitions in limited areas of what might be called "improper" or "unethical" behavior. Some actions which one might consider "improper" or "unethical" do not violate any of the pertinent Rules. An attorney can only be disciplined for conduct that clearly violates a specific Rule. Moreover, this office must assess matters complained of as to whether any potential disciplinary violation involved is established by a preponderance of the evidence. Although we appreciate your frustration as you have described it, because we cannot substantiate a violation of the Rules of Professional Conduct based upon your allegations, we have dismissed the complaints.

At the outset, it is important for you to know some limitations on this office's consideration of the disciplinary complaints. Our jurisdiction and authority is limited to attempting to enforce the Rules of Professional Conduct, a set of minimum ethical standards with which all attorneys must abide. While the Rules are quite broad in their scope, they simply do not prohibit all conduct by an attorney which might be considered as unprofessional, inappropriate, or "unethical."

Moreover, even though you have submitted complaints, this office does not represent you or your personal interests in the PHRC matter. We are not your attorney and cannot provide you with any personal legal advice. We cannot attempt to obtain any remedy or damages you feel you are entitled to nor can we interfere with or intercede in any pending or future legal proceedings you might be involved.

As counsel for the opposing party, the attorneys have a duty to pursue their client's interests, which may naturally oppose your interests. The vast majority of the Rules of Professional Conduct pertain to the attorney-client relationship. The attorneys do not have a duty to you under the Rules such as an attorney would have to a client, including the duty to pursue and protect the interests of anyone other than their client. They are not obligated to act at your direction or in accordance with your demands.

The issues you raise regarding the validity of facts or positions asserted by the attorneys in opposing your complaint before the PHRC involve issues of fact and law that are more appropriate for that tribunal to consider and determine. This office is not the forum in which to challenge the opposing position presented by the attorneys. Thus, your concerns are more appropriately raised before the PHRC or tribunal for review and resolution, not this office.

It is not the role or function of this office to make determinations of law or fact, nor to second guess any such determinations as may be made by a tribunal. Simply put, this office cannot make determinations of law or fact in an underlying matter nor do we have the authority or jurisdiction to impact or otherwise review determinations made by a tribunal.

If you have ongoing concerns, you should consult with counsel of your choosing who can advise you as to any potential rights, remedies, and options you may have to pursue your concerns concerning the PHRC matter.

That said, if in the course of the litigation there is a specific, written finding made by the PHRC or a court that any of the attorneys committed misconduct with respect to the matters about which you complain, you may contact this office at that time and provide

# FORMAL RESPONSE TO THE PENNSYLVANIA DISCIPLINARY BOARD

**Germine Oliver**

October 12, 2024

**Dana M. Pirone**
Intake Counsel
Office of Disciplinary Counsel
820 Adams Ave., Ste. 170
Trooper, PA 19403
610-650-8210

Re: Complaints against
George Charles Morrison, Esquire, (File # C1-24-723)
Andrew Thomas Simmons, Esquire, (File # C1-24-724)
Keith Michael Lee, Esquire (File # C1-24-725)

Dear Ms. Dana M. Pirone,

I am writing to formally express my serious concerns regarding the handling and dismissal of my complaints against attorneys George Charles Morrison, Andrew Thomas Simmons, and Keith Michael Lee. After carefully reviewing the correspondence sent by Ms. Dana M. Pirone on October 9, 2024, it has become clear that the Board's decision to dismiss my complaints reflects significant contradictions, ethical missteps, and a failure to adhere to the standards of impartial oversight that the Disciplinary Board is entrusted to uphold.

The law considers any knowingly false statement made under oath as a serious offense, particularly when it impacts legal proceedings. Under 18 U.S.C. § 1621, perjury can lead to fines and imprisonment for up to five years if proven. The definition includes testimony and written statements presented under oath, where the individual willfully provides false information on a material matter. This can also extend to statements made in written documents if they are submitted with the understanding that they must be truthful, as required in legal settings.

Likewise, making false statements in an official court proceeding or in communications with a tribunal is universally recognized as unethical under various codes of conduct, especially in legal practice. The ethical standards that govern attorneys—such as Rule 3.3 (Candor Toward the Tribunal) and Rule 4.1 (Truthfulness in Statements to Others)—explicitly prohibit this type of behavior. It is not a matter of interpretation or subjective judgment; the rule is clear and objective. The attorneys, by submitting false statements in response to the Pennsylvania Human Relations Commission (PHRC), violated these established rules.

**1. Contradictions in Authority and the Determination of Violations.** The Board's letter claims that it does not have the authority to make factual or legal determinations regarding the case, yet simultaneously concludes that no violation of the Rules of Professional Conduct occurred. This contradiction is deeply troubling, as it raises serious questions about the integrity of the Board's decision-making process.

If the Disciplinary Board lacks the authority to assess facts or evidence, how can it dismiss a complaint based on those very same facts? By claiming both to lack authority and to reach a definitive conclusion, the Board is engaging in circular reasoning, which not only undermines its credibility but also prevents a fair evaluation of the evidence I provided.

Additionally, the letter suggests that I may contact the Board again if a "specific, written finding" of attorney misconduct is made by an external body, such as the PHRC or a court. If the Board is claiming it lacks authority now, why would this change be based on an external ruling? This recommendation further contradicts the stated limitations of the Board's authority and calls into question the consistency and fairness of its approach to enforcement.

**2. Tolerance of Potentially Unethical Conduct.** The letter acknowledges that the attorneys "took a different position" regarding the facts of my case and suggests that their conduct was permissible because they were pursuing their client's interests. While attorneys are obligated to advocate for their clients, they are equally bound by the Rules of Professional Conduct, including Rule 3.3 (Candor Toward the Tribunal) and Rule 4.1 (Truthfulness in Statements to Others). These rules explicitly prohibit attorneys from knowingly making false statements of fact or law.

By framing the attorneys' actions as merely "taking a different position," the Board's letter implicitly tolerates the potential misrepresentation of the facts. This sends a dangerous message—that attorneys can disregard truthfulness as long as it aligns with their client's interests. This attitude undermines the ethical standards that the legal profession is built upon and suggests that the Disciplinary Board is willing to condone behavior that violates the spirit and letter of the Rules of Professional Conduct.

**3. Failure to Address Key Evidence Properly.** The Board mischaracterized the nature of the evidence I provided, treating it as a mere "assertion" rather than verified documentation. Specifically, my formal email request for grade adjudication, submitted on January 24, 2024, was not just an assertion—it was a concrete piece of evidence that directly contradicts the attorneys' claims.

The Board's failure to properly examine or acknowledge this evidence raises serious concerns about the thoroughness and objectivity of the review process. Rule 3.3 and Rule 4.1 place clear obligations on attorneys to act with honesty and transparency. The dismissal of this evidence without investigation reflects a significant failure to enforce these rules, which should have triggered deeper scrutiny into the attorneys' conduct.

**4. Contradictions on Confidentiality and Scrutiny.** The Board's insistence on the confidentiality of the disciplinary process, while typical, takes on an unusual tone in this context. When viewed alongside the contradictions in the Board's reasoning and the implicit tolerance of potentially unethical conduct, the emphasis on confidentiality appears to be more about shielding the Board's decisions from scrutiny than protecting the integrity of the process.

While confidentiality is a procedural norm, it should not be used as a tool to prevent legitimate challenges to the fairness or consistency of the Board's actions. I am fully entitled to discuss how my case was handled under the law, particularly when there are clear indications of bias, ethical missteps, or a failure to enforce the Rules of Professional Conduct.

**5. Erosion of Public Trust and Institutional Integrity.** The Disciplinary Board's role is to maintain the highest standards of ethical conduct in the legal profession. However, the handling of my complaint calls into question whether the Board is fulfilling this responsibility. By failing to thoroughly investigate clear evidence, by issuing contradictory statements about its own authority, and by implying that attorney misrepresentation is tolerable, the Board risks undermining public trust in its ability to uphold the integrity of the profession.

As a body connected to the Supreme Court of Pennsylvania, the Board should hold itself to the highest standard of impartiality and rigor. This is particularly important when dealing with complaints that involve ethical violations that may impact public confidence in the legal system.

**6. Lack of Clear Justification for the Dismissal.** There is no legitimate basis for the dismissal. The letter fails to cite specific facts, legal precedents, or applicable rules that would justify the dismissal. Instead, it relies on vague references to the attorneys "taking a different position" and the Board's supposed lack of authority, neither of which are sufficient grounds for dismissal. Without a detailed and transparent explanation of how the Board reached its conclusion, the dismissal lacks accountability and undermines the entire process. There is no clear, legitimate basis provided for why my complaint did not merit further investigation or review.

**7. Absence of Evidence-Based Evaluation.** The foundation of due process is that decisions are made based on the careful review and consideration of evidence. In this case, there is no indication that the Board engaged in a substantive evaluation of the evidence I provided. Specifically, I noted in my complaint my formal email request for grade adjudication, which directly contradicts the claims made by the attorneys. This email is a key piece of evidence that demonstrates the attorneys' misrepresentation of the facts.

Despite the noted submission to the proper school authorities, the Board's dismissal makes no reference to this email or any other evidence. The decision merely asserts that no violation of the Rules of Professional Conduct occurred but does not explain how that conclusion was reached.

Due process requires that a decision-maker provide reasoning that reflects a review of the facts. Without an explanation as to why the evidence does not support my claims, the dismissal appears arbitrary. The Board's failure to engage with the evidence constitutes a procedural deficiency that undermines the legitimacy of its decision.

**8. No Explanation or Justification for the Conclusion.** Due process demands that decisions be accompanied by a reasoned explanation that connects the facts to the relevant rules. The Board, however, failed to provide any substantive justification for its conclusion that the attorneys did not violate the Rules of Professional Conduct. The letter does not address the key

4

issue of misrepresentation or the contradiction between the attorneys' statements and the documented evidence I provided.

If the Board believed that my evidence was insufficient, it was obligated to explain why. A due process-compliant dismissal would have involved a step-by-step explanation of:

- How the Board evaluated the evidence I provided
- Which specific rules of conduct were applied
- Why did the conduct of the attorneys not violate those rules, based on the facts

The lack of explanation amounts to a denial of due process, as I am left without any understanding of why the Board dismissed my claims.

**9. Contradictions in Authority and Reasoning.** The Board's letter contains contradictory statements that further underscore the lack of a fair process. On the one hand, the Board claims that it does not have the authority to determine facts or review legal issues. On the other hand, the Board dismissed my complaint, which inherently required making factual and legal determinations. This contradiction not only calls into question the fairness of the process but also raises concerns about the legitimacy of the Board's decision.

Due process requires consistency and transparency in reasoning. The Board cannot simultaneously claim that it lacks authority to review facts while issuing a definitive decision that necessarily involves assessing the very facts it claims it cannot evaluate. This inconsistency undermines the credibility of the entire process.

**10. Prejudgment Without a Proper Review.** The dismissal also suggests that the Board prejudged the case without conducting a thorough review of the facts. The conclusion appears to have been reached without properly examining the evidence I submitted, particularly my January 24 email. This gives the impression that the Board's decision was made in a manner that was not impartial or reflective of a full and fair investigation.

Due process requires fair and impartial decisions based on thorough evidence review. By failing to properly investigate the facts or provide an adequate explanation, the Board's dismissal denies me the procedural fairness that is fundamental to the disciplinary process.

**11. Lack of Engagement with the Rules of Professional Conduct.** The Board's letter asserts that the attorneys' conduct did not violate the Rules of Professional Conduct but fails to explain how that conclusion was reached. The attorneys' potential violations of Rule 3.3 (Candor Toward the Tribunal), Rule 4.1 (Truthfulness in Statements to Others), and Rule 8.4 (Misconduct) are key issues that were not addressed in the dismissal.

A proper due process review would:

- Apply the relevant rules of conduct to the specific facts of the case
- Explain why the attorneys' actions did or did not meet the threshold for a violation
- Provide a clear rationale for the decision

The failure to engage with the rules and apply them to the facts in a reasoned manner denies me due process and raises serious concerns about the Board's adherence to its responsibility as an oversight body.

**12. Confidentiality and Suppression of Accountability.** While confidentiality is a procedural norm in disciplinary processes, the Board's emphasis on confidentiality in this context appears to serve as a shield to prevent external scrutiny of a flawed process. Due process includes not only the right to a fair and impartial decision but also the right to challenge procedural deficiencies. By relying heavily on confidentiality while issuing a contradictory and unexplained dismissal, the Board seems to be suppressing transparency rather than protecting the integrity of the process.

Due process cannot be sacrificed in the name of confidentiality. Confidentiality should not be used to obscure accountability, especially when there are clear indications that the dismissal was procedurally deficient and lacked substantive engagement with the evidence.

**Conclusion.** In reviewing the Disciplinary Board's letter, it is evident that the dismissal lacks a valid and justifiable basis. The contradictions in the Board's authority, failure to engage with the evidence, the absence of any substantive application of the relevant ethical rules, and the deferral to other tribunals all point to a decision made without thorough or proper investigation.

The dismissal is not grounded in either fact or law. The Board's reasoning is inconsistent with its role as an oversight body responsible for enforcing ethical conduct standards. This strongly suggests that the decision was not based on a fair evaluation of the merits of my complaint.

Moreover, I must respectfully assert that the Disciplinary Board's dismissal of my complaint constitutes a violation of my right to due process, given that the decision lacks the essential components of a fair and reasonable process. The dismissal of my complaint did not meet the fundamental requirements of due process, given the failure to review the evidence, the absence of a judicious explanation for the dismissal, the blatant disregard for the relevant rules, and the contradictory statements that characterized the correspondence. All these procedural deficiencies suggest that the process was not conducted in a fair or impartial manner.

I am formally resubmitting my complaint with two additional claims that have come to light since the initial filing: 1) the attorneys' false statements regarding their knowledge of my protected activities prior to January 31, 2024, and 2) the false representations made regarding the completion of my required courses. I am also providing new supporting evidence that directly contradicts the attorneys' statements in these matters. These new claims and the associated documentation are critical to understanding the full scope of the ethical violations and provide substantial grounds for reconsideration.

The Board's handling of this matter has broader implications for the enforcement of ethical standards within the legal profession. I hope that the Disciplinary Board will take this opportunity to reaffirm its commitment to fairness, impartiality, and justice. While the Board stressed confidentiality, the dismissal letter has established a precedent, which should not go unchallenged. Therefore, I request that the Board reevaluates its decision and conduct a thorough, but also impartial, review of the evidence and the claims I raised, consistent with the principles of due process. A decision based on the facts, supported by clear reasoning, and grounded in the applicable rules of professional conduct is essential to ensure that justice is served.

In light of the issues outlined above, I formally request a reconsideration of the decision to dismiss my complaints. I urge the Board to conduct a more thorough investigation into the conduct of Mr. Morrison, Mr. Simmons, and Mr. Lee, with full attention to the ethical obligations outlined in Rules 3.3, 4.1, and 8.4 of the Rules of Professional Conduct.

Should the Board choose not to reconsider this matter, I will have no choice but to seek external avenues of accountability to ensure that these ethical violations are properly addressed. My goal is to see this matter resolved in accordance with the ethical standards that govern all members of the legal community. I look forward to your prompt and thoughtful response to this request.

Sincerely,


Germine Oliver


Assisted by Benjamin W. Johnson, Ph.D.

Ben Wood Educational Consulting, LLC
330 W E Main St. #214
Middletown, PA 17057
Phone: 814-424-8816
E-mail: benjaminjson@proton.me


**CC:**
Mr. Thomas J. Farrell, Chief Disciplinary Counsel
Mr. Raymond S. Wierciszewski, Deputy Chief Disciplinary Counsel
Ms. Jana M. Palko, Counsel-in-Charge, Central Intake

# ABOUT THE AUTHOR

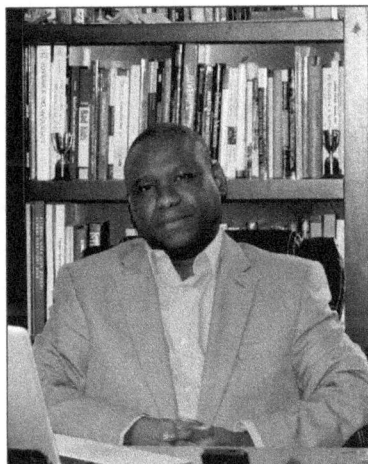

Dr. Johnson is a civil rights advocate, author, educator, and philosopher. He is a social observer. He is also a multidisciplinary researcher. He writes about philosophy, legal theory, public and foreign policy, education, politics, ethics, race, and crime.

Dr. Johnson holds a doctorate in educational leadership, a master's degree in political science, a master's degree in public administration, a master's degree in criminal justice, and a bachelor's degree in criminal justice. He has worked in law enforcement.

Born on April 12, 1975, in Port-au-Prince, Haiti, Dr. Johnson is native French speaker. He is also fluent in many languages, including, but not limited to, Creole, English, Spanish, Portuguese, and Italian. Dr. Johnson enjoys reading, poetry, painting, and music.

# ALSO BY BEN WOOD JOHNSON

Other relevant works by Dr. Johnson

Racism: What is it?

Sartrean Ethics

Jean-Paul Sartre and Morality

Forced Out of Vietnam

Natural Law

Cogito, Ergo Philosophus

International Law

Citizen Obedience

Jean-Jacques Rousseau

Pennsylvania Inspired Leadership

Adult Education in America

Striving to Survive

Postcolonial Africa

www.ingramcontent.com/pod-product-compliance
Lightning Source LLC
Chambersburg PA
CBHW032000190326
41520CB00007B/302